the Open Boat

poems from Asian America

Edited and with an Introduction by Garrett Hongo

ANCHOR BOOKS
DOUBLEDAY
New York · London · Toronto · Sydney · Auckland

An Anchor Book
PUBLISHED BY DOUBLEDAY
a division of Bantam Doubleday Dell Publishing Group, Inc.
666 Fifth Avenue, New York, New York, 10103

ANCHOR BOOKS, DOUBLEDAY, and the portrayal of an anchor
are trademarks of Doubleday, a division of Bantam Doubleday
Dell Publishing Group, Inc.

Acknowledgments for individual poems
appear on pages 301–304.

Book design by Guenet Abraham

Library of Congress Cataloging-in-Publication Data
The open boat : poems from Asian America / edited and with an
introduction by Garrett Hongo. —1st Anchor Books ed.
p.   cm.
1. American poetry—Asian American authors.   2. Asian Americans—
Poetry.   I. Hongo, Garrett Kaoru, 1951–
PS591.A7606   1993
811'.54080895—dc20   92-11089
CIP

ISBN 0-385-42338-1
Copyright © 1993 by Garrett Hongo
All Rights Reserved
Printed in the United States of America
FIRST ANCHOR BOOKS EDITION: FEBRUARY 1993
10 9 8 7 6 5 4 3 2 1

To the memory of Spark Matsunaga,
Poet and United States Senator

Our souls which rise . . .
Are dead to things untrue, unreal.

Editor's Acknowledgments

A compilation like *The Open Boat* is not possible without help, consultation, criticism, and encouragement from a variety of sources. Over a year ago, in a cabin in Volcano, Hawaii, Jeff Masumoto and John Song urged me to initiate this project. From New York, Nicholas Christopher gave crucial practical and professional advice early on. Charles Flowers assisted me capably and expertly from start to finish, performing as researcher and interlocutor, permissions and appendixes editor, and the major contact person for all contributors. Thanks are due to a number of magazine and community newspaper editors whose energies and diligence first brought many of these poets to print in places like *Amerasia Journal, American Poetry Review, Bamboo Ridge, Bridge, Calyx, Chelsea, Contact II, Echoes from Gold Mountain, Greenfield Review, Hawaii Herald, Indiana Review, The International Examiner, The Journal of Ethnic Studies, Kenyon Review, Los Angeles Rafu Shimpo, Missouri Review, The New Yorker, Pacific Citizen, Paris Review, Ploughshares, Poetry, Portable Lower East Side, Quilt, Seattle Review, Yardbird Reader, Y'Bird,* and *ZYZZYVA.* Even as we go to press, I know that *Parnassus: Poetry in Review, Quarry West,* and *Mid-American Review* are compiling issues featuring, in part or wholly, Asian American poets. Publishers like Bamboo Ridge Press, Berkeley Poets Cooperative, Black Sparrow, B.O.A. Editions, Calyx Press, Copper Canyon, Floating Island, Graywolf, Greenfield Review Press, Lost Roads, Shameless Hussy, Station Hill, Story Line, and Wesleyan University Press have each done much to bring out books by Asian American poets. Under its various directors, the National Endowment for the Arts has not only given direct grants to a number of us, but it has also supported publication costs for many of the magazines and small presses just named. In Eugene, Oregon, Cynthia Thiessen, Eugene Gloria, Chang-rae Lee, Tracy Daugherty, Corrinne Hales, and

Shelly Withrow each read and critiqued the initial draft of my Introduction. Mayumi Tsutakawa, Marilyn Chin, Li-Young Lee, David Mura, and Russell Leong also offered important advice on the final manuscript. A conversation with Elaine Kim brought out some very real limitations in my own perspective and reminded me that no one person can be adequate to this responsibility for literary collection and description—there will need to be others. A section of the Introduction was read as part of a panel talk entitled "The State of Contemporary Poetry," delivered in March 1992 at the Poetry Center of the 92nd Street YM-YWHA in New York City. Another section of the Introduction was presented in April 1992 at the Asian American Studies Center at UCLA as part of a symposium entitled "Questions of Identity: Asian American Writers," sponsored by the Academy of American Poets. Finally, I want to give personal thanks to Martha Levin, whose confidence and enthusiasm have fueled my own throughout this project.

About the Editor

Garrett Hongo was born in Volcano, Hawaii, in 1951 and grew up on the North Shore of Oahu and, later, in Los Angeles. He was educated at Pomona College, the University of Michigan, and the University of California, Irvine, where he received an M.F.A. His books include *Yellow Light* (Wesleyan, 1982) and *The River of Heaven* (Knopf, 1988), which was the Lamont Poetry Selection of the Academy of American Poets and a finalist for the 1989 Pulitzer Prize in Poetry. Other recognition includes The Discovery/*The Nation* Award, a Pushcart Selection, and residency grants from the Mac-Dowell Colony and the Bellagio Study Center. He has twice been the recipient of the National Endowment for the Arts Fellowship and was awarded a Guggenheim Fellowship for 1990–91. His work has appeared in magazines such as *Antaeus, The American Poetry Review, Bamboo Ridge, Field, The New Yorker, The Nation,* and *Ploughshares.* He has taught at Houston, Irvine, and elsewhere, and is now Professor of English and Director of Creative Writing at the University of Oregon. For part of each year, he returns to Volcano, where he is at work on a memoir about Hawaii.

Contents

Introduction

I roam America undocumented. . . .
I am all ready,
    my belongings wrapped in a bundle. . . .
        —from *Songs from Gold Mountain*

You did not give America to me, and never will.
America is in the hearts of the people that live in it.
But it is worth the coming, the sacrifice, the idealism.
        —Carlos Bulosan

"If I am going to be drowned—If I am
going to be drowned, why in the name of
the seven mad gods who rule the sea, was
I allowed to come thus far and contemplate
sand and trees?"

        —Stephen Crane

At the December 1990 meeting of the Modern Language Association in Chicago, the Asian American Literature Study Group sponsored a late afternoon reading entitled "Asian American Writers of the Midwest," featuring poets David Mura and Li-Young Lee and fiction writer Kyoko Mori. There were over one hundred and fifty people in attendance then, among them many of the leading scholars in the new field of Asian American literature along with some of the most eminent younger poets in the country. Long before the start of the reading, an expectant throng filled the middle-sized meeting room and, if one arrived late, dashing from another panel as I was, there was only room enough to stand. About half in attendance were Asian Americans. The crowd was abuzz and electric in mood in the way I've come to know means authority, power, and joy—as if a new community was in the process of bringing itself together. I stood among many friendly faces, nodding to them, and tried to gauge the prestige of the moment, casting my mind back to only four years before when, at a similar MLA event, there were only a scant forty or so attending, almost exclusively scholars in the field of Asian American Studies. Things had changed and I wondered if I could believe that the change had been overnight.

The reading was momentous and, soon after, it was reported so in the Sunday *New York Times Magazine*. Amidst all the intellectualism of the annual meeting of the profession, amidst a sea of Aristotelian rhetoricians and poststructural semioticians, the *Times* reporter cited this one panel of Asian Americans as the single moment of eloquence and human wisdom she appreciated most. It was gratifying to me, hearing about it afterward, far away from university life on academic leave back in my home village in Hawaii, that the *Times* had come to report on it at all. That it had chosen to feature the reading and praise it for its vibrancy, its note of passion, was more than amazing and, I thought, historically significant. Things had indeed changed.

· · ·

Gannen-mono. Paper son. *Manong. Pau hana. Gum sahn.* Mountain of Gold. *Tengoku*. Illegals. Labor contract. *Kanyaku-imin*. Ticket dance. Runaway. Picture bride. Chinese Exclusion Act. Executive Order 9066. "I Am Chinese." Flips. *Juk sing.* ". . . fight to prove our loyalty." F.O.B. No-No Boy. Manzanar. The Golden Spike. ". . . your slanty-eyed, Korean ass. . . ." Citizenship. Chinatown. Assimilation. Heritage. Homeland. Gooks. Boat People. "Success Story: Outwhiting the Whites." Hmong quilt. The "Community." Ancestors. Vincent Chin. Homeland. Hawaii Calls. HR 442. *haiku*. Pantoum. *Cababayan*. Greengrocer. Cleaners. Dogeaters. Diploma. Diaspora. Asian American. Song, Encarnacion, Shahid Ali. Ai. *Aiiieeeee! The Woman Warrior*. Bruce Lee. Immigration attorney. Kearny Street. International Hotel. Berkeley quota. Wharton School. Chancellor. Tenure. One-and-a-half. Mainland. Homeland. "Third-generation return." Immigrant. Sojourning. "So Long, Oolong . . ." *Kung-Fu*. Fuck you. "Say Hello to Uncle Sam." Postcolonial Amirthanayagam.

. . .

Above is the word-cloud that I wrote to begin thinking about how to account for all that follows in these pages. For the thirty writers here emerge out of more than a hundred years of immigration, sojourning, settlement, misconception, stereotyping, and soul-searching that each has turned into the special singing we call poetry. Though descended from immigrants from Asia, most of us are American-born, learned English as a native language, went to American schools, and forged identities which had to negotiate the tricky, volatile, and, ultimately, to my mind, *exciting* subjectivized space between race and culture. We come to consciousness aware of the history of immigration and the Asian diaspora, singing from the fissures and fragmentations of culture in order to bring about their momentary unity in the kind of evanescent beauty that the figure of a poem makes. Born to a politically shifting and postcolonial world, we emerge out of a generational diversity as well, some born before World War II, many in the postwar baby boom, and some even in the sixties. We are born in exotic places like Boston, Sri Lanka, Honolulu, San Francisco, Pasadena, Jakarta, and Chicago. At the moment, we live in mundane places like Manhattan, Eugene, Arcata, Seattle, Santa Fe, and Taipei. We are teachers, community organizers, intellectuals, freelance writers, students, and editors. One manages business holdings. One is a greengrocer. As poets, we have established ourselves in diverse regional, ethnic, or academic identities, reading to audiences in San Francisco's Glide Memorial Church and at The Poetry Center of the 92nd Street Y in New York, in the grand ballroom of the Chicago Hilton and in an immaculate classroom building at McCarty's Trading Post at Acoma Pueblo in New Mexico. Our books are published by small presses, regional presses, ethnic and women's presses, university presses, and New York commercial presses. We write about violence to women, about the paintings of Utamaro and Willem de Kooning, about plantation workers and picture brides, about factory work and the pleasures/dangers of sex. We write about our Eurasian children. We *are* Eurasian. And Afro-Asian. One of us can write out of strongly held Christian religious convictions instilled by a refugee, theologian father who preached in a small town church in Western Pennsylvania, and another from a grounding in French semiotic theory, poststructuralist cultural critique, and American postmodernist art criticism. One voice could have the feeling and flavor of Hawaiian pidgin, a creole English, and another echo, in its rhetoric, the smoothness of Mallarmé's French or mirror the *bric-a-brac* of Frank O'Hara's pop art lunch poems.

But can it be fairly judged who is the cosmopolitan and who the provincial? We each come from a linguistic margin and a cultural center. Or, as Yogi Berra says, *vice versa.* We are of the diaspora. Americans. We write about food and family, about what we hold sacred and what we deem profane. If there is a commonality to our work, it exists, to varying degrees, around our own recognition of history and our private dialogues, magically romantic or existentially uneasy, with the consciousness of race in America.

If I count back from the first Chinese contract laborers brought to work the California gold fields and westering railroads, there is an historical foreground to this poetry that is perhaps more than a hundred years long. If I count back to the *gannen-mono*—the first Japanese laborers brought to work the cane fields of Hawaii in 1878 —it is also over a hundred years. Filipinos and Koreans came very soon after that—also largely as contract laborers—and then, beginning at the end of the nineteenth century and continuing through the beginning of the twentieth, a trickle of Asian professionals and other educated workers began to immigrate as well. After World War II, a change in immigration laws, and the slow removal of federal and state statutes specifically excluding or limiting Asians, the Asian immigration diversified as did the class and purpose of the immigrants. Though the pioneering groups had come largely to do unskilled agrarian labor, the groups after mid-century came to do urban labor and included many urban professionals. Most recently, Asians have arrived from Hong Kong, Taiwan, Kampuchea,

Thailand, Viet Nam, Laos, Singapore, Malaysia, Indonesia, India, Korea, Mexico, Peru, Trinidad, Jamaica, Cuba, Canada, and the Philippines. They already have children who were born Americans and who have been reading some of the poets in this book.

. . .

> My husband cuts the cane,
> I do the *hore hore*.
> By sweat and tears
> We get by.
> —*hore-hore bushi*

> Identity is crucial to ideology and action—central to the problem of self-determination at any level.
> —Franklin Odo, Preface to
> *Roots: An Asian American Reader*

In the seventies, when I was a college student (in English) in California and then a graduate student (in Japanese literature) in the Midwest, I was forever fighting the stereotype, the dehumanized image of Asians in America, the *invisibility* of our historical, social, and cultural presence in this country. When I took time away from my academic commitments during my junior year to join with other Asian American students to form an association and sponsor cultural events—we wanted to invite speakers on Asian American history, we wanted to bring the Sansei poet Lawson Fusao Inada to give a reading, we wanted to be part of a Third World Students' Cultural Festival, and we wanted an Asian American dance party—my professors, though kindly, twitted me for "Asian Americking" and "going ethnic" on them.

My new commitments to ethnic awareness and cultural activism seemed threatening to the collegiate society around me. I was speculating, but I wondered if my bright, eupeptic, and pipe-smoking white male professors from Yale and Berkeley worried I might go the route of radicalism and Angela Davis (a visiting professor my sophomore year), the route Leroi Jones took in becoming Amiri Baraka, rejecting the Beats and Zenophiles who were his former friends in Greenwich Village and embracing Newark, Coltrane, and the Black Arts Movement. I groped to contextualize my wish to explore Asian American identity and to learn our history. I wanted to swim in the slipstream.

An Irishman and a Jew, both from Los Angeles, helped me out. Writers and scholars, they taught me about the Celtic Revival and the Irish literary Renaissance, the poets of Negritude and the Spanish Civil War, the American poets against the war in Vietnam. They taught me about nativist and recuperative literary movements, about ethnic revivals and precedents in seeking alternative traditions even as one wrote from within the historical context of colonized or dispossessed peoples. They taught me about *alterity*.

My Asian American classmates doubted literature and Asian American identity could make a field of study, let alone a life, but they helped me find books like *Longtime Californ'* (Pantheon, 1973) by Victor and Brett de Bary Nee; *Roots: An Asian American Reader* from UCLA (1971); *Factories in the Fields* (Peregrine, 1971) by *The Nation* editor Carey McWilliams; and *Concentration Camps, USA* (Holt, Rinehart, and Winston, 1971) by relocation historian Roger Daniels. I found Lawson Fusao Inada's *Before the War: Poems as They Happened* (Morrow, 1971), at that time the first and only collection of poetry by a Japanese American. I found black novelist Ishmael Reed's ground-breaking, multiethnic anthology *19 Necromancers from Now* (Doubleday, 1970), containing "Goong Hai Fot Choy," a moving piece of fiction by Frank Chin. The piece was a chapter, the headnote said, from *A Chinese Lady Dies,* a yet unpublished novel set in San Francisco's Chinatown. Written in a stately and cadenced prose, it featured a striking tenderness in the relationship between a coming-of-age Chinese American man and his dying mother— something so deeply *human* it was revolutionary at that time. No one had yet accomplished the full creation of Asian American subjectivity in literature. I tried writing my first poems about figures in my own family—plantation workers in the cane fields, labor organizers leading strike marches at the beginning of this century, a teenage girl singing lullabies to her adopted younger brother in mixed Japanese, Hawaiian, and English. I wrote out of a growing sense of our Asian diaspora, a history of dispersion and a culture of *bricolage.*

"You can't make a living," a Chinese American classmate said. "You gonna go broke tryna write abou' dat." He was from Terre Haute, Indiana, the son of a storekeeper, and is now an economist for the OMB. "Who's gonna read abou'd us?" I remember him saying, again and again, "Nobody *real* gonna care."

What he meant was that the mainstream, what we thought of as "America" and the conceptual norm of citizens and any potential readership, was going to be white, middle-class, and uninterested in us, our fractured histories, our emerging identities full of fissures and unjoined psychic seams. Whatever America was, it would be uninterested in its own margins and our job was rather to find our way into some kind of centrality either of economics or of culture in order to secure a presence, to earn and protect a standing in this country. America was, in the main and, ultimately, to this mindset, essentially *white,* inviolably white. It was *The Donna Reed Show* and *Father Knows Best.* It was "Western Civ" and Erasmus and Descartes and Shakespeare and Gilbert and Sullivan. Asians were bit players, extras with buck teeth and pigtails on TV shows like *Bonanza* and *Kung Fu.* We were Charlie Chan, Mr. Moto, and Joe Jitsu. Or, we were Plum Blossom and Suzie Wong—exotic and docile beauties catering to the sexual pleasures of white men. We were *not* real, but cartoons and caricatures, sideshows and servants, jokes in a Jack Nicholson movie and ciphers of the mainstream culture contributing nothing generative and original of our own, but adding "spice" to the melting pot. If we emerged at all, we had before each of us a mask of the dehumanized and stereotyped image of Asians in our American culture. Slanted eyes, simian features, servile personalities. And, whether we laughed or wept from joy, moaned or were silent from grief, it would matter not at all to the *real* of experience, of literature, of culture in America. We were canceled. An absence. The *real* was owned externally to any identity we might possess or try to create. The *real* is what canceled us, made us absences, even to ourselves.

If I found any precedent for an Asian American literati, he would have to be a bit player. Sansei political scientist Daniel Iwao Okimoto (a man with degrees from Princeton, Harvard, Tokyo, and Michigan), predicted this in his autobiography, *American In Disguise* (Weatherhill, 1971), contrasting himself unfavorably to literary giants of non-Asian ethnicities like Bernard Malamud, John O'Hara, and James Baldwin. Considering Okimoto's discouraged, self-castigating statements, I thought of predecessors like Eurasian Sadakichi Hartmann, who was secretary to the retired Walt Whitman (who called him, once, "that damned Japanee"), camp follower of silent-screen swashbuckler Douglas Fairbanks. Sadakichi was a trickster who wore coattails and a top hat, a lorgnette like W. B. Yeats, wrote "jottings" and aphorisms about East and West collected at UC Riverside and brought into print by amateur Orientalist Kenneth Rexroth as literary amusements under the title *White Chrysanthemums* (Herder & Herder, 1971). When I visited the Riverside library, I found stunning photographic portraits of a brooding Sadakichi taken in New York by Alfred Stieglitz. I realized Sadakichi had been part of things, part of the cultural revolution that became Modernism, part of the center.

Slowly, an alternative truth was being made available to us, we first- second-, third-, and even fourth-generation children of immigrants from Asia. We learned from a handful of scholarly books and study materials then being developed in Asian American Studies Programs at UCLA, San Francisco State, Cal State Long Beach, and Berkeley. We learned about the Asian Exclusion Laws of the late nineteenth century that limited Chinese immigration to single men and forbade interracial marriages. We learned about the Alien Land Laws of the early twentieth century that forbade Japanese immigrants from owning land. We learned about the Chinese workers who built the western sector of the Transcontinental Railroad and then were excluded from the photograph of Americans who drove the Golden Spike. We learned about their massacre in Wyoming. We learned about yellow journalism, the Hearst papers, and the editorial campaigns against the "Yellow Peril" our Asian ancestors represented to white labor and management. We learned about Filipino laborers in the salmon canneries of Alaska, in the produce fields of California and apple orchards of Washington. We learned about the tradition of small Japanese American truck farms along the California coast and Central Valley. We learned about the history of farm and plantation laborers, about Koreans and Filipinos in the ILWU. We learned about the great Filipino American writer Carlos Bulosan, who went from colonial childhood in the tracks of a carabao ploughing a rice paddy, to youth in labor camps and beet harvests in the American West, to an adulthood of labor activism and literary writing. Chapters of his inspiring autobiography, *America Is in the Heart* (Harcourt, 1946), were originally published in *The New Yorker*. We learned about Executive Order 9066, Franklin Delano Roosevelt's decree excluding all persons of Japanese ancestry from the West Coast of America after the spring of 1942 in the aftermath of Pearl Harbor, and the wartime hysteria against the Japanese spilling over into an officially enacted persecution by the government of a people by reason of race. We found photographs of the periods. We found documents. We found Chinese poems carved into the walls of detention cells and benches on Angel Island in San Francisco Bay and we translated them. We found English and Japanese poems written in the World War II concentration camps in the western deserts and published in a camp magazine called *Trek*. A Nisei housewife once handed me a sheaf of her poems. They were imitations of the Master's exam list in English poetry made up by Stanford critic Yvor Winters that his wife Janet Lewis sent to her when she was a teenage girl in camp at Poston, Arizona. We heard our grandmother singing an old song she remembered from the plantation days in Kahuku, a *hore-hore bushi,* a worker's tune from the cane fields. We reprinted all of them in our student newsletters and our new Asian American literary magazines. We learned the history of racism against Asians in America. We learned the fractured and fissured histories of a variety of Asian peoples who, all of us, had become Americans and lived a piece of a larger story none could tell alone. We learned the *real* and began to give our testimony.

Aiiieeeee!: An Anthology of Asian American Writers, originally published by Howard University Press in 1974 and then reprinted by Anchor/Doubleday in subsequent paperback editions, was the catalytic and seminal anthology of the new Asian American literary consciousness. Though historically not the first Asian American literary anthology—there were others edited by Chinese-born Kai-yu Hsu and Taiwan émigré David Hsin-Fu Wand—this volume edited by playwright Frank Chin, poet Lawson Fusao Inada, short story writer Jeffrey Paul Chan, and novella artist Shawn Wong— all American-born—was by far the most influential one, documenting an intriguing and stimulating record of literary publication among Japanese, Chinese, and Filipino Americans from the prewar period until the contemporary. Though it excluded poetry, *Aiiieeeee!* collected memoir, drama, and fiction from three generations of Asian Americans culled from publication in the ethnic vernacular presses, academic literary quarterlies, the script archives of regional theater companies, and fresh manuscripts written for ethnic studies and creative writing classes. Furthermore, it identified and argued for, in a strongly worded and hectoring introduction, a native-born Asian American literary *language* and sensibility that was not Oriental or Western European, but a native development of American culture. In their introduction, the editors of *Aiiieeeee!* did the brave and innovative job of performing a persuasive and memorable critique of the history of racism in American literature and popular culture, liberating a younger generation of writers from under the domination of the stereotype and instigating new creative vision and activity.

The seventies was a fervent time for Asian American writing. Not only were there Equity-waiver productions of original Asian American plays going on at places like the East-West Players in Los Angeles, A.C.T. and the Asian American Theater Workshop in San Francisco, and the Asian Exclusion Act in Seattle, but there came into being several new magazines devoted to Asian American literature. *Bridge* was a community arts magazine that grew out of energies originating from The Basement Workshop in New York's Chinatown. Its focus was Asian American identity in the arts, and it published the writings of and feature articles on singer-songwriters Joann Miyamoto and Chris Iijima, a review of musicologist Charlie Chin's rock revival group Cat Mother and the All Night News Boys, the poetry of San Francisco community activist Janice Mirikitani, and interviews with several Asian Americans in film, drama, and other arts. I read it everywhere, even once on a streetcar in Kyoto, Japan, in 1973 when an acquaintance from Arkansas handed it to me, saying, "Read this poem." It was "my ship does not need a helmsman" by Alan Chong Lau, and it was the most moving thing I'd yet read by anyone of my own generation.

I had not then met Lau, but within a few days I made it a point to. It happened he lived in Kyoto then, and we made a friendship out of exile, poetry, and a shared need for Asian America. He gave me a copy of *Aion,* the magazine out of San Francisco State edited by Janice Mirikitani. "She gives these readings in Nihon-machi, man," Lau said, sipping his *genmai-cha,* "And she does it with *taiko* drummers and *odori* dancers, you dig. And the people, they *turn* out!" The issue in my hand had an abstract, reddish, *bizen-yaki*-like cover, and its interior pages featured the finely wrought and subdued, cool-jazz poetic work of Lawson Fusao Inada from Fresno, California, who had lived as a child in the Jerome, Arkansas Relocation Center. From college, I had written to Lawson, and he'd sent me a first-edition copy of John Okada's *No-No Boy* (Tuttle, 1957), the first Japanese American novel, then out of print. I tucked it into a map-pocket of my backpack so I could have it with me sojourning in Japan.

In the mid-seventies, when I got back, the American Place Theater got on to public television a production of Frank Chin's Chinatown drama entitled "The Year of the Dragon." *Yardbird Reader,* a ground-breaking west coast literary and arts magazine edited by Ishamel Reed and devoted to Third World writers, gave over its third issue exclusively to Asian American writing edited by Frank Chin and Shawn Wong. The Oakland Art Museum was sponsoring the first Asian American Writers' Conference in 1975. At Yale University in 1971, students Lowell Chun-Hoon and Don Nakanishi had founded *Amerasia Journal,* a scholarly pamphlet dedicated to publishing research in the new field of Asian American Studies. It included academic papers on educational statistics of Asian American schoolchildren, academic review articles, oral histories from San Francisco's Chinatown, and, once in a while, a poem or two. Later that year, the magazine moved to the Asian American Studies Center at UCLA where it grew into a substantial scholarly quarterly and continued to publish weighty academic articles and occasional literary features. Twice it published special literary issues, gathering together fiction, memoir, poetry, and reviews by Asian American writers of several generations. In 1976, UCLA Asian American Studies Center also published *Counterpoint,* edited by activist Emma Gee, the second large compendium of Asian American scholarly and literary material. Also in 1976, I edited a special Asian American issue of *Greenfield Review* published in conjunction with the Pacific Northwest Asian American Writers' Conference in Seattle at the University of Washington. "And the Soul Shall Dance," Wakako Yamauchi's sorrowful lyric drama of farm life among Japanese Americans before the war, became an East-West Players hit in Los Angeles in 1977 and was filmed and broadcast for public television in 1978–79.

All of this was extraordinary activity, yet, perhaps the single most important event for Asian American writers in the mid-seventies was the publication and subsequent popular acceptance of Maxine Hong Kingston's *The Woman Warrior* in 1976. The literary achievement and commercial reception of the work was unprecedented in the brief but fervent literary history of Asian America. Subtitled "Memoirs of a Girlhood Among Ghosts," it stimulated popular attention for the private experiences of an Asian woman in America and gave a portrait of a mythological consciousness that seemed capable of empowering untold numbers of women and, potentially, any silenced "other" of our culture, no matter what the background. For *The Woman Warrior* broke strenuous cultural silences about women's identity and Chinese American identity, resituating racial and gender consciousness in historical and mythological *alterities* imagined out of folklore, family history, and private meditation. In one part of the book, Kingston proposes a culturally purgative heroine, a re-imagining of Fa Mu Lan, the woman warrior of Chinese legend and history, who left her dying village to become general of a great army, then, once revenge was accomplished, transformed herself back into her identity as woman and mother. In another part, she tells the story of a Chinese Procne or Hester Prynne, a "No-Name Woman" raped by an unnamed neighbor, ostracized by her village, who commits suicide by throwing herself down a well after her bastard child is born. Kingston re-imagines the *topoi* of Western and Asian cultures, gives them new situations, magically real, and the cloak of a marvelously poetic prose style. With the emergence of Maxine Hong Kingston on the best-seller lists, the television talk shows, and, eventually, her work collected in high school and college textbooks and assigned as part of standard curricula, American culture had a new kind of writer—the *Asian American* writer. The literary decade which had begun on a note of brash machismo with the liberating outcry from the editors of *Aiiieeeee!*, thus ended on a deeply plangent note of powerful feminist independence and literary vision from novelist Maxine Hong Kingston.

. . .

During the eighties, numerous Asian American poets began to publish, at first in journals having to do with ethnic studies, then almost simultaneously in university quarterlies and the slicks too, some even producing full-length collections with literary and commercial publishers. By the mid-eighties, I'd twice been asked to edit anthologies of Asian American poets. I hesitated and, ultimately, declined these editing opportunities, feeling that an anthology then would face too many political and aesthetic challenges, not the least of which was the problem of my own lack of a confident perspective. I had too much of my own writing work to accomplish, I felt, and collecting the poetry of my peers and predecessors could stand a little waiting.

Yet, the audience and the poets kept maturing and changing, and three dramatic events came together in 1991 to help me decide to put together *The Open Boat*. "Shaping the Legacy: The Asian American Writers' Conference" in February at UC Berkeley opened a fervent and collegial dialogue for me with other Asian American poets at the same time as it made clear the need for a strong critique of the available interpretative approaches to our burgeoning literature. Then, news of the successful lawsuit against Copyland/Kinko's by minority writers who were members of Oakland PEN sensitized me to the widespread practice of xerox pirating of our work by numerous university ethnic studies programs. Finally, two young Asian American poets from Berkeley and UCLA visited me in my home village in Hawaii and spoke to me of their feeling for our work and their wish to know more about us, to see our work collected together in a literary context, to find out about Asian American poets they hadn't yet come across in ethnic studies courses.

A kind of secondary system of literary authority *within* Asian

America had arisen since the early seventies, you see, through the ethnic presses, university ethnic studies programs, vanguard student groups, and community arts centers that had, although unconsciously and uncritically, created a profile of what the Asian American writer was supposed to be. Roughly, the profile was this: the Asian American writer was an urban, homophobic male educated at a California state university who identified with Black power and ethnic movements in general; he wrote from the perspective of a political and ethnic consciousness raised in the late sixties; he was macho; he was crusading; he professed community roots and allegiances; he mocked Eurocentrism and eschewed traditional literary forms and diction in favor of innovation and an exclusively colloquial style; his identity was stable and secure, a personification of a specific geographic region and an ethnic ethos; and, though celebrated in the Asian American "movement," his work was widely unrecognized by "the mainstream." For a while, the culture's main critical response to the provisional paradigm was to erect a *macha* counterpart. But things had changed since this profile had been put together, and it needed to be critiqued, overturned, feminized, or, at the very least, made much more complicated. Instinctively and critically, the student organizers of the Berkeley conference were able to recognize this. They brought together a new generational group of writers with a diversity of strong literary voices from all over the country and allowed us to meet each other and begin exciting dialogues.

Included in the event were writers who, to my perception, had been up until that time consistently *excluded* from Asian American literary venues for one reason or another. I was excited to be reunited with a few participants I expected—Janice Mirikitani, Elaine Kim, Jeff Tagami, Joy Kogawa, and others familiar from the Asian American movement of the seventies. But I also met John Yau, the Chinese American poet who is a postmodernist art critic and had been a student of John Ashbery's. I met Cynthia Kadohata, the Sansei novelist who had written *The Floating World* (Viking, 1989), a beautifully lyric novel about an eccentric family of Japanese Americans who drove from job to job across the South and Southwest during the fifties. She confessed she'd come expecting to be attacked by other Asian American writers as, during her West Coast promotional tour the year before, a vulgar few who professed community loyalties had criticized her book as being "unrepresentative." When I walked up and introduced myself to her, praising her work, she was astonished. She'd expected a confrontation and none came. I had a reunion with the stylishly New Age and intellectual poet David Mura from Minnesota, who had visited me in Hawaii two years before. He was writing exceedingly brave and sophisticated poems about race, the Relocation, and sexuality that, in their stichic and sequential structures, reminded me of the essayistic verses of Auden. I met a thoughtful Arthur Sze, the poet whose translations of Tu Fu and Li Po I'd been reading since 1972, whose finely tuned, reflective lyrics seemed to me partitas of compassion and consciousness. This was an extraordinary and provocative event, and I was glad to have been a participant.

. . .

I hear America singing, the varied carols I hear . . .
—Walt Whitman

Today, there are four major realities that dismantle the older, culturally biased model of the Asian American writer. First and most obviously, it is impossible to construct a universal profile out of the thirty-one poets in the following pages. And who would want to? Certainly not the poets themselves. Second, novelists Maxine Hong Kingston and Amy Tan, two feminist women, are, by far, the most famous and popularly accepted Asian American writers. Third, David Henry Hwang, a witty and urbane graduate of Stanford, writer of sprightly and caustic Broadway hits like *M. Butterfly*, is perhaps the most well-known Asian American *male* writer. Finally, the place of Asian American poetry in relationship to what is culturally perceived and constructed as "the mainstream" has dramatically changed.

With the eighties and on through the nineties, there has been empowerment and a demonstrable rise in the recognition of works by Asian American poets. Cathy Song's *Picture Bride* won the Yale Series of Younger Poets competition in 1982. John Yau's *Corpse and Mirror* (Holt, 1983) was selected by John Ashbery for the prestigious National Poetry Series. The Academy of American Poets honored Ai, me, and Li-Young Lee with their Lamont Poetry Selections for 1978, 1987, and 1990. Three of us have been awarded Guggenheim Fellowships, several with NEA Fellowships, two with Wallace Stegner Fellowships, and not a few with The Discovery/*The Nation* Award from The Poetry Center of the 92nd Street Y. Bamboo Ridge Press in Honolulu, partially supported by NEA grants, published collections by Eric Chock and Wing Tek Lum. In 1989, Calyx Press in Oregon published *The Forbidden Stitch: An Asian American Women's Anthology,* edited by Shirley Geok-lin Lim and Mayumi Tsuta-kawa. Gerald Stern, senior poet of the Iowa Writers' Workshop, selected David Mura's *After We Lost Our Way* (Dutton, 1989) as a winner of the National Poetry Series competition. These days, some of us even serve on foundation and NEA panels, sit on national awards juries, teach in and direct academic creative writing programs, and edit literary magazines. A couple of us appeared with television journalist Bill Moyers on "The Power of the Word," his 1989 PBS miniseries of interviews with contemporary American poets. We are included in the textbook and annual anthologies published by Norton, Heath, McGraw-Hill, Little Brown, Morrow, Godine, St. Martin's, Pushcart, and Scribner's.

Yet, for all of this progress, there are obstacles. It is still left for us, as a new generation of writers, to provide cultural interpretations from a variety of perspectives. This is an imperative. Without it, there is an abyssal void that can only be filled with the passionate intensities of an outdated message. Because, for all this common ground in questions of ethnicity and identity, there have been problems and a serious ideological battle within the field known as "Asian American literature." In its short history, it is my feeling that the category has been all too narrowly defined to include the wide range of diversity in all of the published works. While we, as Asian American writers, probably share, by degrees, some understanding of the history of Asians in America, it is arguable whether or not we can agree on an identifiable model for the *culture* of Asians in America from which we must derive our work. Yet, some have argued exactly that and argued vociferously, seeking to define our Asian American literature into two fundamental categories—authentic and inauthentic.

At the Berkeley conference, its aesthetic inclusiveness and diversity notwithstanding, there was, to me, a troubling consistency of interpretation that kept cropping up in various conversations, at the panels, and at the open forum workshops with students and other registrants. Students, journalists, scholars, and activists in attendance continually spoke of our varied works as if they were written by one, politically radical, socially relevant, filially pietistic master writer. There seemed to be an interpretive theory in place that *flattened* significant differences among Hawaii's Eric Chock, Hong Kong–born/Iowa-educated Marilyn Chin, and East Village postmodernist John Yau. We were celebrated, in fact lavished with attention, yet the applause seemed to be for someone else and not for us—someone who writes for an idealized fiction called "the community" and is governed by a wish for a predominantly political or sociological construction of Asian American identity.

Late in the conference, after a dinner party that was followed by a marathon poetry reading, I made the observation that our works weren't so much read as our appearances and personalities were *interpreted*—and then along fairly simple lines of social image and racial pride, sociological themes of ethnicity, and political iconoclasm. At the hotel the next morning, I recall making the complaint (I complain a lot) to fellow conferees—five of us had just checked out and were waiting in the lobby for rides to the airport—that we weren't so much listened to as intellectuals, as employed as ritual objects of the culture. "We were *samurai* and *geisha* dolls inside of glass boxes, man," I said. "Decorations to add prestige and provide evidence for the *ideological* constructions being produced by our appearances." And what were those ideological constructions?

There seemed to be three dominant modes out of which critical thinking about our creative activity emerged: (1) an unconscious assumption that what was *essentially* Asian American was a given work's overt political stance and conformity to sociological models of the Asian American experience, (2) the related notion that a writer writes from a primary loyalty to coherent communities, and (3) vehement castigation or rude, categorical dismissal for literary qualities deemed "assimilationist" or "commercial." It was, to me, significant that Bharati Mukherjee and Maxine Hong Kingston, members of the Berkeley faculty and writers of complicated fictions, were not invited to participate in the conference.

A vocal and influential few, not there in attendance at Berkeley but now elsewhere disseminating their views widely in the culture, are chained to the traits of bitterness and anger in the previous model of the Asian American writer. They have alleged that recognition is itself a sign of a given writer's personal assimilation of an insidious bourgeois culture and a corruption of that which is the "authentic" literary culture of Asian America—something which stands defiantly and belligerently apart from the world of mainstream American letters. They have engaged in the ideological practice of judging the cultural pertinence of a given literary work by employing a litmus test of ethnic authenticity. The test works this way—if a work is adjudged meritorious by any American institution that can be characterized as "mainstream," then that work must necessarily be "inauthentic" in terms of Asian American culture and, therefore, is due for condemnation by loyalists and exclusion from the reading lists of Asian American or Ethnic Studies courses. This practice, to me, is nothing more than fascism, intellectual bigotry, and ethnic fundamentalism of the worst kind. It is entirely a shame, as Salman Rushdie recently pointed out (I saw him on C-SPAN, a televised press conference at The Freedom Forum of The American University), that "the description of one's work can fall largely into the hands of one's enemies." It is also entirely a shame that few Asian American Studies scholars have been willing to publicly condemn and seriously critique this arch and ingenious twisting of cultural interpretation.

Ethnic pride and an acceptance of our history do not necessarily militate against liberalities of thought. A critique of the vacuities and impediments to a freed consciousness under bourgeois culture does not necessarily mean an abandonment of intellectual tolerance. Political awareness, engagement, and commitment do not oblige us to conform to rigid constructions of ethnic identity, to accept prohibitions of consciousness decreed by cultural guardians full of journalistic thunder or in fearful possession of curricular control. The powerful human wish for a community of affection cannot restrict our literary expression (or even our critical thinking) to conform to whatever might politically be constructed (or captured) as community will.

Literature, whatever else it is, has forever been available as a protest against domination—by the ruling class, by the family, by the father, by the former regime, by the mind-set of the group—even a group that is traditionally one's own. There is an assuredly positive value to the public politics of ethnicity—I do not want to forget or undervalue any of our movement roots—yet the process they take in constructing meaning and identities for their participants is primarily social and results in a meaning and identities which are also primarily social. It is literature's function, as a special case in human activity (it is *art,* after all), that its process is *not* social and that the meaning it constructs is primarily a subjective, even a dissident truth. The wounded singer leaves the fireside and celebrating tribe in order to brood on the blood scars in her soul and scarrings of those her tribe has defeated, returning to the circle days later with a wise and plangent song of triumph over woe. The cane worker sings *hore-hore bushi* in a complaint of hardship and gives his soul surcease from his body's pain.

At this historical moment, the issues surrounding Asian American poetry (and perhaps the literary construction of ethnicity in general) could be characterized as a generational conflict between those who wish to uphold the notion of a personal subjectivity and poetics *within* the American experience, minority or mainstream, and those who make their priority the production of a polemicized critique of generalized ideological domination within our culture. These are not perspectives which must *necessarily* be incompatible in and of themselves, but there has been a problematic tendency, manifested in the critical practices of some few invested with public influence and institutional authority, to hegemonize the variety of projects within the field known as "Asian American literature" which has resulted in the privileging of some of the most polemical and parochial approaches to literary production.

By contrast, many here in *The Open Boat* may have some ambition to widen the interpretive field of whatever might be called "Asian American literature," to oppose canonical orthodoxies, to resubjectivize and vivify existing sociological interpretations and exclusively materialist models of our experiences, and to encourage diversity, intellectual passion, and an appreciation of verbal beauty. It may be that we seek a kind of serious bewilderment that clarifies experience. Yet, few would want to be prescriptive about literary creativity, proscriptive about style or theme or perspective. Being doctrinaire is not a requirement for inclusion in this anthology. Publication can itself be an avenue toward liberation. It is thus that writers reach out from our inner lives of agonistic contemplation to the lives of a charitable, sympathetic spirit wished for by our readers.

For the thirty-one poets included here, our own individual literary odysseys differ and diverge. They may have taken some of us through community or women writers' workshops, and some will have spent significant time in Asian American writers' groups. We may have established our unique voices in some solitude and isolation, or, perhaps more commonly these days, we may have spent time in a graduate creative writing workshop at an academic institution. Our influences could derive as much from the poetry of the English Renaissance, from Modern scholarship on T'ang Dynasty Chinese poetry, from admiring the landscape odes of Rabindranath Tagore, from trash-talking and signifying on the streets of the Mission District in San Francisco, or from engaging in heady, theory-laden discussions of the contemporary movement known as language poetry. Each poet defines for us a world, and those worlds are as varied as the dreams of ten thousand saints imagining ten thousand worlds, each with their heaven and hell, each made of emptiness and with form.

. . .

I was glad. I felt inspired. Yes, there was music
in me, and it was stirring to be born. I wrote for
the night, subsisting on coffee and bread.
Carlos Bulosan,
America Is in the Heart

I've never been in Peking, or in the Summer Palace,
nor stood on the Great Stone Boat to watch
the rain begin on Kuen Ming Lake, the picknickers
running away in the grass.

But I love to hear it sung . . .
—Li-Young Lee

For me, one voice among so many others, a voice I've tried to train as much out of a passion for English and American poetry as out of my loyalties to the Japanese American past of four generations and to the landscape of Hawaii, the place of my birth, it has been a *feeling* for language and its beauty that has brought me to poetry and kept me at it. I enjoy the sound of the language raised in quiet passion, the finish of sentient attention on a line of free or formal verse, the rich patina of elegant syntax and coloraturas of dense accentuals sliding into the syncopated rhythms of common speech. To me, our American poetry is a Memphis of languages—a place named for an ancient capital that sits at the confluence of rivers and cultural slipstreams. One can hear in it the Afro-American bassline of field hollers and the blues, in influences derived from the Anglo-Scot gospel tradition, in the small-town balladries of love lost and won, and in the echo, quiet or loud, of the Norton anthology and the greater tradition behind any contemporary innovation.

Like musicians and traditional singers, the poets I admire most love to make a sound and perhaps love making it as much or more than any creation of what used to be called meaning, more than striking the show-colors of cultural allegiance. They gather these in the meeting place that is a language of lavish exchange. I hear the insistent choruses of Miles Davis's "So What" in the rhythmic, striding lines of Lawson Fusao Inada. His words have the timbre of ecstasy and transport, of tenderness and rage. They have, of course, the force of history and a highly developed personal consciousness, but they partake as much to me of a tradition of sacred speech, heightened speech—a reverence for power, precision, and beauty in language. One hears vernacular vocabulary and syntax ordered and filigreed through dithyramb and repetition into chant and variation something like the energetic jazz-sonata convention of post-bop theme, improvisation, and chorus.

Our contemporary poetry, the best of it, teaches and encourages us that there is a glory and splendor in us, that delight is in our languages and in our capacities to be susceptible to them, to be moved by them. We might hear of the infinite and the sublime in insinuation and nuance at first, a "catch in the throat" as Robert Frost once wrote, but it is finished and brought into our culture through the Stevensian phaetons of energy and insight he called the noble rider and the sound of words. I love this poetic "vibrato," the excess of beauty and attention, this Sensurround of *artificiality* that, to me, makes for the most moving and beautiful poetic language. If there is something to me that I would call the salient characteristic of poetry—contemporary or otherwise, Donegal or Singapore English, songs from a Kearny Street Pinoy or sonnets from a South Hadley, Massachusetts Yank—I'd say it was this *sprezzatura* of consciousness and sound I feel in my bones and my throat and my breast and my loins when I hear or read the work that moves me and turns me gay, yet fills my eyes with tears.

It is perhaps difficult to make a poetry from that emotional catch in the throat, that which compels us to speak when so much passion swells that, out of pride, the act of speaking is what we might fear the most. But our poets speak anyway, raising voices in the most beautiful way we know how, fitting passion to the traditions of song that quell passion in the singer at the same time as they might raise passions in those sung to. It seems to come in cadences that can be counted out if the poet is formally trained and sufficiently in love, or it can come freed of the strict metric yet following alternative orders of ceremony like the psalmodic lyrics of the Bible and the Book of Lamentations, the Night Chant of the Navajo, the Pindaric ode-forms of traditional Hawaiian gospel music, signifying street tales, or the little verbal rondo that a sestina by Elizabeth Bishop makes. There is a powerful delight in all of these and all of these are poetry to me. Here my statement is nearly done. "I will arise and go now, and go to . . ." Ohwhyee.

> "If I am going to be drowned—if I am going to be drowned, why in the name of the seven mad gods who rule the sea, was I allowed to come thus far and contemplate sand and trees?"
>
> —Stephen Crane

On March 4, 1992, the Academy of American Poets in conjunction with the Rockefeller Foundation, the Ford Foundation, the Lila Wallace–*Reader's Digest* Fund, and the Nathan Cummings Foundation sponsored a panel talk at The Asia Society in New York City featuring four Asian American writers—Jessica Hagedorn, David Mura, John Yau, and me. The moderator was Dr. Shirley Hune, past president of the Association for Asian American Studies who is now Vice Provost and Professor of Social Foundations of Education at Hunter College, CUNY. The panel was the initial event of a year-long national symposium on Asian American writing that will also take place, with varying lineups of writers, in St. Paul, Minnesota; Los Angeles, California; and Honolulu, Hawaii.

The symposium idea originated with William Wadsworth, Executive Director of the Academy, who wanted to hold a national celebration of the work of living Asian and Asian American poets. Late in 1990, he wrote to me in Hawaii, asking for help designing the symposium and orchestrating its events. It took the 1991 Berkeley conference to help me crystallize my decision to be involved, seeing that it was the right thing, that it was the right time.

At The Asia Society that night in New York, four of us read briefly from our work and held a spirited discussion calling for a moratorium on exclusively sociological interpretations of our work and for a critique of essentialist theories of race and culture. We took questions from an earnest, lively audience. People remarked on our camaraderie, how easy we seemed to be with each other, that it was apparent that we *liked* each other. There were season ticket holders, influential editors, and academy and foundation officials in attendance, but the largest part of the audience we spoke to was made up of students, scholars, and writers, many of whom were young Asian Americans. There were poets there from academic programs at NYU, Stanford, Columbia, UCLA, Berkeley, Swarthmore, and Wisconsin. There were street poets and slam poets and performance artists. I was told that a group of young writers from Chinatown, conspicuous for their flashy dress and cohesiveness, took up an entire row of plush Asia Society seats all by themselves. We want to reach all of them. We hope our work speaks to them. We do not wish to speak *for* them.

It is a plain fact that recognition has come to us and to our work as part of the American voice that is great within us. We are already upon the shore of the land, though, undeniably, there have been losses and lands left behind. We will not forget them. We join in a movement of voices that may have spoken its first words in a language of Asia or, just as likely, in the language of Anne Bradstreet and Dickinson, Heavy D. and Whitman, Crane and Jean Toomer, Frost and Gertrude Stein, Elvis and W. S. Merwin. The people are running and shouting on the grassy hills above the strand where the wreckage of a boat bounces in foaming surf higher than our knees. We lift our voices, bodies from the sand, and call.

—Garrett Hongo
Eugene, Oregon

the Open Boat

Ai

Edward Putzar

Ai is a native of the American Southwest. Her first book, *Cruelty,* appeared in 1973. Her second book, *Killing Floor,* was the 1978 Lamont Poetry Selection of the Academy of American Poets. Her third book, *Sin* (1986), won an American Book Award from the Before Columbus Foundation. Her fourth book, *Fate,* appeared in 1991.

The Man with the Saxophone

New York. Five A.M.
The sidewalks empty.
Only the steam
pouring from the manhole covers seems alive,
as I amble from shop window to shop window,
sometimes stopping to stare, sometimes not.
Last week's snow is brittle now
and unrecognizable as the soft, white hair
that bearded the face of the city.
I head farther down Fifth Avenue
toward the thirties,
my mind empty
like the buddhists tell you is possible
if only you don't try.
If only I could
turn myself into a bird
like the shaman I was meant to be,
but I can't,
I'm earthbound
and solitude is my companion,
the only one you can count on.
Don't, don't try to tell me otherwise.
I've had it all and lost it
and I never want it back,
only give me this morning to keep,
the city asleep
and there on the corner of Thirty-fourth and Fifth,
the man with the saxophone,
his fingerless gloves caked with grime,
his face also,
the layers of clothes welded to his skin.
I set down my case,
he steps backward

to let me know I'm welcome,
and we stand a few minutes
in the silence so complete
I think I must be somewhere else, not here,
not in this city, this heartland of pure noise.
Then he puts the sax to his lips again
and I raise mine.
I suck the air up from my diaphragm
and bend over into the cold, golden reed,
waiting for the notes to come,
and when they do,
for that one moment,
I'm the unencumbered bird of my imagination,
rising only to fall back
toward concrete,
each note a black flower,
opening, mercifully opening
into the unforgiving new day.

The Shadowboxer

You know what hunger is, Father,
it's the soothing half-dark
of the library men's room
and the reference librarian,
his head pressed against my thigh
as tears run down his pudgy face.
Sometimes I unzip for him
and let him look,
but never touch, never taste.
After all, I'm here to try to reconcile
the classics
with the Batman-comics philosophy of life,
and this pathetic masquerade,
this can't be life in caps or even lower case.
This is 1955, and all I know is boredom and desire,
so when I leave, I cruise down Main Street
for girls and a quick feel.
They call it the ugliest street in America,
but I don't know yet
that it's just another in a lifetime of streets
that end kissing somebody's feet or ass.
I just tell myself to drive and keep on driving,
but like always, I swerve into our yard.
You're still at Henrahan's,
drunk and daring anyone to hit you,
because you're a man goddamnit.
I climb the stairs to my room
and lie down under your boxing gloves,
hung above my bed
since your last fight in Havana.
When I can't sleep,
I take them down, put them on,
and shadowbox, until I swing,

lose my balance, and fall,
and on the count of six
you rise off the canvas,
only to be knocked backward into the ropes,
sure that half your face
flew out of the ring,
but it was only blood flung
like so much rum from a glass
into all the screaming faces,
into one woman's face
as she stands
and leans into the next spray of blood.
Do it, she cries
as she raises her fists, *do it.*
Bathed, stitched, and taped together,
you manage to dress
and get halfway to the street door
before you feel her
behind you in the darkness primeval,
but when you call, nobody answers
and you're twelfth floor up
Hotel Delirious
with Billie Holiday on the hi-fi.
Don't explain, she sings,
and the rum on the night table,
for the sweet dreams
it never really does bring, sings back, *Do,*
as you perform your latest attempt
to escape you, Father,
and what happened one night
when I stopped believing
even in the power of money to absolve.
Remember?
The first time I had a woman,
I even called your name. You didn't answer,
but you do answer the three short knocks,
and my mother, Rose,
still wearing her blood-spattered clothes,

crosses the threshold.
Turn back before it's too late, I tell her,
as she peels the tape off your face,
licks and kisses your wounds,
then mounts you
and plunges you deeper each time,
crying, *Show me what a good man can do,*
and you, Father, you,
rocking with her
until you must slow her, must ease her off
and stanch the blood above your eye.
Can you feel me, Father, breaking into a run
down conception road,
nothing but nasty business on my mind,
just two steps ahead
of all the bloody noses,
the broken bones
and blackened eyes you'll give me?
Nobody believes the lies you tell,
but they want to
and that's enough.
It's tough without a mother,
but fatherless is tougher on a boy, they say.
Nobody sees how twisted up I am
or how squeezed dry of anything resembling love.
I loved my mother,
but she left us to our few feet of deep space
for the hard chest and thighs of a comer,
the postcards she sent now and then from Venezuela,
Australia, even Paris,
reminding you of what you want to forget,
and when your good eye lingers on your son,
all you see is one more reason to hit him.

.   .   .

Then one night, you stagger to my room.
I don't resist when you slap and kick me.
Faggot, you scream
as you tear my T-shirt and shorts off me,
I heard about the library.
Then, then, you rape me.
You're snoring when I pack gym bag
and take the boxing gloves
and stuff them in with my underwear
and Old Spice soap-on-a-rope.
I don't know where I'm going,
I just go as far as I can,
which in the end is Bellevue Detox,
is suddenly the smell of Gleason's gym—
men's sweat,
men's armpits, crotches,
men's wins and losses,
all that's left of Rosy Jack, Jack Rose,
middleweight loser
and sometime trainer of other losers mostly
or movie stars
and novelists who think the fights are glamorous,
who want to get in touch with themselves
by hitting someone else,
or for a "serious" role,
but I tell them
it's really all about a boy
finally beaten to submission.
Although he's crying *More,*
because he's been taught to think
he deserves to be punished,
he doesn't hear himself
as he locks the door
to keep his father in the wretched past
where he belongs,
but the past is now,
is you, Father, in this corner
and me in mine, stripped

to your level at last,
as the bell sounds
and the crowd bites down
on its collective tongue,
when the first punch stuns me
and the second knocks me all the way
to kingdom come and gone.

Agha Shahid Ali

Isabelle Bize

Agha Shahid Ali, a poet from Kashmir, earned his Ph.D. from Pennsylvania State University and his M.F.A. from the University of Arizona. He has won fellowships from the Pennsylvania Council on the Arts, Bread Loaf Writers' Conference, and the Ingram Merrill Foundation, among others. He has published a book of criticism, *T. S. Eliot as Editor* (UMI Research Press, 1986), a book of translations of the noted Urdu poet, Faiz Ahmed Faiz, *The Rebel's Silhouette* (Peregrine Smith Books, 1991), and two books of poetry, *The Half-Inch Himalayas* (Wesleyan, 1987) and *A Nostalgist's Map of America* (W. W. Norton, 1991). Currently, he is an Assistant Professor at Hamilton College.

A Lost Memory of Delhi

I am not born
it is 1948 and the bus turns
onto a road without name

There on his bicycle
my father
He is younger than I

At Okhla where I get off
I pass my parents
strolling by the Jamuna River

My mother is a recent bride
her sari a blaze of brocade
Silverdust parts her hair

She doesn't see me
The bells of her anklets are distant
like the sound of china from

teashops being lit up with lanterns
and the stars are coming out
ringing with tongues of glass

They go into the house
always faded in photographs
in the family album

but lit up now
with the oil lamp
I saw broken in the attic

.   .   .

I want to tell them I am their son
older much older than they are
I knock keep knocking

but for them the night is quiet
this the night of my being
They don't they won't

hear me they won't hear
my knocking drowning out
the tongues of stars

A Dream of Glass Bangles

Those autumns my parents slept
warm in a quilt studded
with pieces of mirrors

On my mother's arms were bangles
like waves of frozen rivers
and at night

after the prayers
as she went down to her room
I heard the faint sound of ice

breaking on the staircase
breaking years later
into winter

our house surrounded by men
pulling icicles for torches
off the roofs

rubbing them on the walls
till the cement's darkening red
set the tips of water on fire

the air a quicksand of snow
as my father stepped out
and my mother

inside the burning house
a widow smashing the rivers
on her arms

Cracked Portraits

My grandfather's painted grandfather,
son of Ali, a strange physician
in embroidered robes, a white turban,
the Koran lying open on a table beside him.

I look for prayers
in his eyes, for inscriptions
in Arabic.
I find his will:
He's left us plots
in the family graveyard.

   . . .

Great-grandfather? A sahib in breeches.
He simply disappoints me,
his hands missing in the drawing-room photo
but firm as he whipped the horses
or the servants.

He wound the gramophone to a fury,
the needles grazing Malika Pukhraj's songs
as he, drunk, tore his shirts
and wept at the refrain,
"I still am young."

   . . .

Grandfather, a handsome boy,
sauntered toward madness
into Srinagar's interior.

In a dim-lit shop he smoked hashish,
reciting verses of Sufi mystics.
My father went to bring him home.

As he grew older, he moved toward Plato,
mumbling "philosopher-king,"

Napoleon on his lips.
Sitting in the bedroom corner,
smoking his hookah, he told me
the Siberian snows
froze the French bones.

In his cup,
Socrates swirled.

   . . .

I turn the pages,
see my father holding a tennis racquet,
ready to score with women,
brilliance clinging to his shirt.

He brings me closer to myself
as he quotes Lenin's love of Beethoven,
but loses me as he turns to Gandhi.

Silverfish have eaten his boyhood face.

   . . .

Cobwebs cling
to the soundless
words of my ancestors.

No one now comes from Kandahar,
dear Ali, to pitch tents by the Jhelum,

under autumn maples,
and claim descent from the holy prophet.

Your portrait is desolate
in a creaking corridor.

(for Agha Zafar Ali)

Homage to Faiz Ahmed Faiz
(d. 20 November 1984)

> "You are welcome to make your
> adaptations of my poems."

1

You wrote this from Beirut, two years before
the Sabra-Shatila massacres. That city's
refugee air was open, torn
by jets and the voices of reporters.
As always, you were witness to "rains of stones,"

though you were away from Pakistan, from
the laws of home which said: the hands
of thieves will be surgically
amputated. But the subcontinent always spoke
to you: in Ghalib's Urdu, and sometimes through

the old masters who sang of twilight
but didn't live, like Ghalib, to see the wind
rip the collars of the dawn: the summer
of 1857, the trees of Delhi
became scaffolds: 30,000 men

were hanged. Wherever you were, Faiz, that
language spoke to you; and when you heard it,
you were alone—in Tunis, Beirut,
London, or Moscow. Those poets' laments
concealed, as yours revealed, the sorrows

of a broken time. You knew Ghalib was right:
blood must not merely follow routine, must not
just flow as the veins' uninterrupted
river. Sometimes it must flood the eyes,
surprise them by being clear as water.

2

I didn't listen when my father
recited your poems to us
by heart. What could it mean to a boy

that you had redefined the cruel
beloved, that figure who already
was Friend, Woman, God? In your hands

she was Revolution. You gave
her silver hands, her lips were red.
Impoverished lovers waited all

night every night, but she remained
only a glimpse behind
light. When I learned of her,

I was no longer a boy, and Urdu
a silhouette traced
by the voices of singers,

by Begum Akhtar, who wove your couplets
into ragas: both language and music
were sharpened. I listened:

and you became, like memory,
necessary. *Dast-e-Saba,*
I said to myself. And quietly

the wind opened its palms: I read
there of the night: the secrets
of lovers, the secrets of prisons.

3

When you permitted my hands to turn to stone,
as must happen to a translator's hands,

I thought of you writing *Zindan-Nama*
on prison walls, on cigarette packages,

on torn envelopes. Your lines were measured
so carefully to become in our veins

the blood of prisoners. In the free verse
of another language I imprisoned

each line—but I touched my own exile.
This hush, while your ghazals lay in my palms,

was accurate, as is this hush that falls
at news of your death over Pakistan

and India and over all of us no
longer there to whom you spoke in Urdu.

Twenty days before your death you finally
wrote, this time from Lahore, that after the sack

of Beirut you had no address . . . I
had gone from poem to poem, and found

you once, terribly alone, speaking
to yourself: "Bolt your doors, Sad heart! Put out

the candles, break all cups of wine. No one,
now no one will ever return." But you

still waited, Faiz, for that God, that Woman,
that Friend, that Revolution, to come

at last. And because you waited,
I listen as you pass with some song,

a memory of musk, the rebel face of hope.

Indran Amirthanayagam

Tom Lyles

Indran Amirthanayagam is a Tamil from the Jaffna peninsula in northern Sri Lanka, although he spent much of his childhood in Sri Lanka's capital, Colombo. Born in 1960, he received a B.A. from Haverford College and an M.A. in journalism from Columbia University. He is now a poet, teacher, and theater critic living in New York City. His poems have appeared in *Grand Street, The Kenyon Review, The Massachusetts Review*, among other journals. His first collection of poems, *The Elephants of Reckoning*, has just appeared from Hanging Loose Press (1992).

The Elephants Are in the Yard

I see the elephants in the yard
Pappa, the white snake too
peering out of the neem tree's trunk
hissing poisons

Pappa, I see the wild boar
in the thicket, the branches
burning with his smell, Pappa
bring out your gun,

I want to eat the boar's meat
and stare at his head
on my wall, Pappa I see
the elephants in the yard

The partridge and jungle fowl
you shot from the air and bush
to conquer alone
the harvest of the jungle

You were always a sport
took on bird in flight, boar
in fierce charge, your life or his
I see the elephants in the yard

and poachers cock-eyed
devouring their tusks in dreams
building grand compounds
massing riches in stainless steel

Pappa, the sport is finished
the elephants are in the yard
and there is no forest
and there are lots of knives

. . .

and forks and tractors
and babies to feed
and guerrillas hiding
in the shade of neem and mango

right there beyond the verandah,
in the center of the garden
where your dowry will build
your last daughter's house

the elephants spread their heavy bodies
tired from the journey up country
and down country, the long herding,
to some safe peaceful house.

There Are Many Things I Want to Tell You

There are many things
                I want to tell you,
how in the lamp night
red candles light your hair,
how in the day, the Sun
like your father kisses
your three year old ear,
and your heart and wings flutter,
you spread your arms
in a white gown, a bird
smiles and sleeps in the air,

as you do now,
as you lie before me,
and I take my arms out
into the wind,
and gather sands and trees,
           robins and jasmine;

There are many things
                I want to tell you,
how I walked in Jaffna town,
arm in arm with you,
and my mother ran from the verandah
out into the street, and my father got
down in a lilac suit from the Austin,
and we met and drank tea,
and read Dickens, and ate mutton—
while the palmyrah gave us shade
and Tamil lent us proverbs.

. . .

There are many things
                    I want to tell you,
about sun-rich holidays
of morning fish and sea pools,
pianos playing in the drawing room,
Lucky holidays where money did not matter,
and I woke up, a terrier
after a deep sleep, and yapped
at mangoes at jack fruit,
eating like a hog,
a well-mannered fatted hog—
nothing wrong with eating,
said the Roman priest, my teacher,
in the snooze of the afternoon;

There are many things
                    I want to tell you,
how in the churches
the lower castes sat
on the floor, the high
        on benches,

There are many things
we need to do, I want to tell you,
to give every boy and girl
the finest school books
and the loveliest hearts to read
in Tamil, English and Sinhalese,
to help the outcast:
find rice and wood,
a wife or husband,
swim in rain water pools
for hours, or play cricket,
or live as a hermit
and read the ancient scriptures;

.   .   .

There are many things
                    we could do together,
attend the graduation
of the ten thousandth woman doctor,
give alms to the crowd
that has met for peace,
a federal agreement
for Ceylon or Lanka,
help arm the revengers
of innocents fix accounts in the Earth,

so the Earth can drive
to the party in heaven,
in a fine cloak of snow,
a dress of mangoes
for love-making,
a cheek slapped, yet strong
like a ten thousand year old oak;

There are many ways
to get ready for the party:
sit in a silent room
and rest your spirit,
fly from land to land,
picking fruits and wines,
pigments to paint boys and girls,
touch your skin
with my skin,
so our skins will melt—

like snow in the Sun,
like blood
when onions trade South
again, or North,
or East, or West,
like a boy
dancing with a girl,
twenty seven years young
and not seen a dead body yet,

. . .

like a man and woman
roped in a pit—
tied in arms and legs,
surrounded by heads
chopped off on platters—

who melt into water,
who steam into the Sun,

like molecules
in the cell of Heaven,
who meet and dance
at The Party of the New.

So Beautiful

So beautiful that couple
in handsome black and red clothes
walking along the street
her arms folded, his in pockets cold . . .
Scarves loosely wrapped about white necks,

And in the subway car
a black man takes a black woman's hands,
and her eyes look far away
beyond the walls under the sea,

and his eyes concentrate on her hands
as glasses drop slightly down his nose
as she turns and smiles, as he looks up
at clay made whole,

and she takes her hands about his cheeks
makes a vase, and he smiles
as roses are put in his mouth and hair,

and her brown leather coat crumples
as she kisses him,
and his black windbreaker is crumpled
by her kiss,

And for two subway stops their kiss
moves a man to write
and get up in the morning
and sing an old song

to remember a woman in a dream
who held his hands
wearing ear rings of white moons,
in black hair open as a fan,

. . .

blowing honeyed wind about the room
in which they loved and loved,
as kingdoms came and went,
in which they loved and loved

as the black man and woman
left their embrace
to slowly get up to the door
by an old man in the window seat
into whose hands dropped two white moons.

Mei-mei Berssenbrugge

Dorothy Alexander

Mei-mei Berssenbrugge was born in Beijing, China, in 1947, and grew up in Massachusetts. She has a B.A. from Reed College and an M.F.A. from Columbia University. Her most recent books are *The Heat Bird* (Burning Deck Press), which won a Before Columbus American Book Award, and *Empathy* (Station Hill Press, 1989), which won the PEN/West Award in Poetry. She lives with her husband, the artist Richard Tuttle, and their daughter in New Mexico.

Chronicle

I was born the year of the loon
in a great commotion, My mother—
who used to pack $500 cash
in the shoulders of her gambling coat,
who had always considered herself
the family's "First Son"—
took one look at me
and lit out again
for a vacation to Sumatra.
Her brother purchased my baby clothes;
I've seen them, little clown suits
of silk and color.

Each day
my Chinese grandmother bathed me
with elaboration in an iron tub;
amahs waiting in lines
with sterilized water and towels
clucked and smiled
and rushed about the tall stone room
in tiny slippers.

After my grandfather
accustomed himself
to this betrayal by First Son,
he would take me in his arms,
walk with me
by the plum trees, cherries, persimmons;
he showed me the stiff robes
of my ancestors and their drafty hall,
the long beards of his learned old friends,
and his crickets.

. . .

Grandfather talked to me, taught me.
At two months, my mother tells me,
I could sniff for flowers,
stab my small hand upwards to moon.
Even today I get proud
when I remember
this all took place in Chinese.

The Constellation Quilt

She stitched her story on black
silk patches from the mourning dress, quaint
as our novels will seem, but we still recognize
tonight's sky, as if there were a pattern
whose edges compose with distance, like nebulae
or namings, so triangles become Orion
Horse, Morning Star, not flanks and wings imagined
in gases, or story pieced out of intervals
from which any might grow, as if sparks ever
scattered the same, or a name assume one face
and stance, dated in cross-stitch in a corner
Stitching a name like defoliate in white thread
on white fabric leaves the leaf empty. In that
century, it was a giraffe or a bear's act. Sometimes
the only pattern seems shock waves advancing
in parallel fanned lines, leaving a tide's debris
whose pattern is moon, cryptic as if there were none
the one safe assumption. Littlest sisters eclipsed
are each another story of a marriage, using the same
scraps for different constellations, Bear, Swan
overlapping

Tan Tien

As usual, the first gate was modest. It is dilapidated. She can't tell
which bridge crossed the moat, which all cross sand now, disordered with footsteps.
It's a precise overlay of circles on squares, but she has trouble locating
the main avenue, and retraces her steps in intense heat for the correct entrance,
which was intentionally blurred, the way a round arch can give onto a red wall,
far enough in back of the arch for sun to light it.

If being by yourself separates from your symmetry, which is
the axis of your spine in the concrete sense, but becomes a suspension
in your spine like a layer of sand under the paving stones of a courtyard
or on a plain, you have to humbly seek out a person who can listen to you,
on a street crowded with bicycles at night, with their bells ringing.

And any stick or straight line in your hand can be your spine,
like a map she is following in French of Tan Tien. She wants space to fall
to each side of her like traction, not weight dispersed within a mirror. At any time,
an echo of what she says will multiply against the walls in balanced,
dizzying jumps like a gyroscope in the heat, but she is alone.

Later, she would remember herself as a carved figure and its shadow on a blank board,
but she is her balancing stick, and the ground to each side of her is its length,
disordered once by an armored car, and once by an urn of flowers at a crossing,
because Tan Tien is a park, now. The stick isn't really the temple's bisection around her,
like solstice or ancestor. This Tang Dynasty peach tree would be a parallel levitation
in the spine of the person recording it.

Slowly the hall looms up. The red stairway's outline gives way to its duration
as it extends and rises at a low angle.
In comparison to the family, the individual hardly counts, but they all
wait for her at a teahouse inside the wall.
First the gold knob, then blue tiers rise above the highest step,
the same color as the sky.

When one person came to gain its confidence,
she imagines he felt symmetry as flight after his fast among seven meteorites
in the dark. He really felt like a globe revolving within a globe.

Even the most singular or indivisible particle or heavenly sphere will adjust
when the axis extending beyond itself is pushed, or the sphere it is within
is pushed. What she thought was her balance flattens into a stylized dragon
on the marble paving stones.

Yet she's reluctant to leave the compound. Only the emperor
could walk its center line. Now, anyone can imagine how it felt
to bring heaven news. She is trying to remember this in Hong Kong
as the tram pulls suddenly above skyscrapers and the harbor
and she flattens against her seat, like a reversal occurring in the poles,
or what she meant by, no one can imagine how.

Jealousy

Attention was commanded through a simple, unadorned, unexplained, often decentered presence,
up to now, a margin of empty space like water, its surface contracting, then melting
along buried pipelines, where gulls gather in euphoric buoyancy. Now,
the growth of size is vital, the significance of contraction by a moat, a flowerbed, or
a fenced path around the reservoir, its ability to induce the mind's growing experience of the breadth
and depth of physical association, which turns out to be both vital and insufficient, because
nature never provides a border for us, of infinite elements irregularly but flexibly integrated,
like the rhythm between fatigue and relief of accommodation, or like a large apartment. Now,
the construction is not the structure of your making love to me. The size of your body on mine
does not equal your weight or buoyancy, like fireworks on a television screen, or the way
an absent double expresses inaccuracy between what exists and does not exist in the room
of particular shape, volume, etc., minute areas and inferred lines we are talking about.
You have made a vow to a woman not to sleep with me. For me, it seemed enough
that love was a spiritual exercise in physical form and what was seen is what it was,
looking down from the twelfth floor, our arms resting on pillows on the windowsill. It is midnight.
Fireworks reflected in the reservoir burst simultaneously on the south and the north shores,
so we keep turning our heads quickly for both of the starry spheres,
instead of a tangible, and an intangible event that does not reflect. Certain
definite brightness contains spaciousness. A starry night, like a fully reflecting surface,
claims no particular status in space, or being of its own.

The Swan

He calls it their stage, which echoes our first misrecognition of unity. Instances
of false unity, he calls the imaginary, and he locates in them sites of her dreams,
out of which she is able to want him. The way stage lighting can be a story by itself, now
she makes time for a story, not coming from her or her coming from her story, but both from before,
seeing a flock of birds fly up from a frozen pond, while you stand in the wind, instead
of hearing wind about to arrive across a huge space, so that her train passes a lagoon
in Connecticut, *and* she sees swans swimming at the edge of ice piled against the shore, feminine swans.
Remembering what I heard you say and fixing my desire for you simultaneously, a meaning
of instability, not hesitance, holds you *and* the swans accountable for making the desire,
although the meaning of the desire existed prior to being desired.

Truth effects produced within a dream, neither true nor false in themselves,
operate through repetition to convey an illusion of truth or meaning,
which may be the constant sum of varying systems of dreams, like birds startling from a cottonwood tree
and wind about to arrive, or your seemingly high standards for truth, considering that
where femininity is concerned, similar effects yield various meanings, as when a woman photographed
on two separate occasions on the street at random by a famous photographer, who's dead now,
still finds herself in a purely theoretical relationship with herself in relation to him,
which he refuses to merge with the intermediacy of real light. That immaterial matter truly
leaves objects their own places, lighting and illuminating them. Therefore,

she pays attention to absurd and trivial details where her desire dissolved, among
all sorts of things that happened, both in the present and in general, so her focus on absurdity appears
to be a spontaneous part of the desire itself, where coincidence and nonsense merge in a lover,
until the sky would look on you as a composite of video monitors on surfaces slowly disintegrating
into ice swans which resemble, for example, an opera house.

Finally, one must sort of drop one's reserve, which could be a kind of definition
of physical beauty, without which no transformation takes place, such as
if you were a mother, the interval between the child and you. This is analogous
to her own physical beauty. It dominates, but does not determine its own content
or its experience, because the dream was not a concept but a means of generating experience,
so that the mother and I desire, but the child is a desire, in spite of the child being physical.

. . .

A flock of birds flying up acquires the shape of her arcs across the ice, a mirror stage,
echoing our first misrecognition or the imaginary, to look again and then look,
so that if he says or she says, my dream about you is older than my knowing you,
does that mean the dream was dreamed before your meeting him or her?
The meaning of the dream existed prior to the dream, and then I met you and then I dreamt about you,
gratifying an enigma that was solved and then posed, with a resulting fullness
in the dreamer, as with a child to replace himself or replace herself, or as verisimilitude on stage.
Its story is light that moves from cue to cue as over ground.
It resembles an arm reaching out to defend you at a sudden stop, but is rhetorical,
the way your arms full of white down inscribe an immense volume above the ice.

Edmond Yi-Teh Chang

Yiwen Chang

Edmond Yi-Teh Chang was born in Taipei, Taiwan, in 1965, and lived in Taiwan and Libya prior to coming to the United States in 1980. He graduated with honors from Tufts University with a B.A. in history and international relations. He spent a year as a poet-in-residence at St. Andrew's School in Delaware, followed by a year studying at the writing program in Houston, before receiving his M.F.A. from the University of Iowa's Writer's Workshop in 1991. Presently, he is pursuing a Ph.D. in comparative literature with particular emphasis in classical Chinese poetry. His awards include an Academy of American Poets College Prize while at Tufts, an Inprint Fellowship and Mitchell Scholarship while at Houston, and a Graduate Fellowship from the University of Iowa.

After the Storm

Muskrats rose from the marsh
flooded from yesterday's rain.
I stood at the kitchen window
watching them prowl in my garden,
stripe-faced demons,
tails stiff in the wind.
They're gone this morning,
everything a mess out there,
turnips dug out and carved,
beans, peppers, broccoli flowers
maimed and scattered in dirt.
The crop of my bowels.
Each day I'd squat
with my dress pulled up
to nourish them, my knees
clicked at the joints.
I don't say much anymore.
My voice is weak.
Years ago they killed
my son in Motor City.
Is that not enough loss
for a woman to bear?
Why should I plant new seeds?

In memoriam Vincent Chin
(1955–1982)

Bamboo Elegy: Two

Each night with moist leaves
          gathered from teapots
I stuffed his mouth to kill the stench.
          I wrapped fresh strands
of kelp around him to slow the rotting.
          It was the last days
of our crossing, 1866 I think,
          reign of T'ong-tze,
the queue then hanging from my head
          down to the waist.
He had died from fever after only
          two weeks at sea.
I lay him in the corner with the monkeys.
          I didn't cover his face.
I didn't throw him in the sea as they asked.
          He looked pitiful,
the same look I remembered seeing on his face
          in that bamboo grove,
lying against a rock reading some romance.
          He was in tears.
What shame! The fool! I trample down
          the walls of bamboo.
In my head, I saw only her small shoulders,
          how delicately she squatted.
I watched her wash my brother's shirts
          on the river-bank.
In bed his body was the widest body between us.
          The sun's last glint
on the water never made me more daring.

. . .

The day we landed
I buried him in a grave on the cliff
            overlooking the ocean.
I didn't dig very deep, the ground was hard,
            lupine growing everywhere.
I tore some up by the roots, yellow ones,
            to toss in his grave.
The wind made the wild grass swim
            around the pit.
Like those fallen buds I'd see sometimes
            spinning in a whirlwind
of peanut shells and dust near my feet
            when I'm at the park.
It was not the California I promised him,
            flowers over his face,
dirt in his mouth, in his ears.
            How does one measure
the distance each shovel of dirt makes?
            I cut off my queue,
placed it on his chest, cut off his to keep.
            What could I have told her?
That I convinced him to come here knowing
            he wouldn't make it?
That I left him under a bent cypress, thinking
            I could dig him up
in a year or two, sail home to Taisan
            with his bones,
buy out the neighbors, tear down the grove.
            That I wanted cash crops
like lychee and betel palm. Black pigs
            feeding on cassava,
feeding on tender shoots breaking ground.
            I saw black beetles
scuttling over his grave, black crows
            on the cypress.
I brought him persimmons that day,
            my last visit.

. . .

I watched the inland breeze ferry the lupine
in waves out to sea.
There was no need to worry, I was leaving
for the Sierra Nevadas.
Out there, a life was waiting to be found.

Near-Sightedness

In fall, when afternoons begin
to melt quickly into night,
when billboards and street signs
blur in the distance, I'm reminded
again of my failing eyes,
of the gradual obscuring of things.
I've tried eating more carrots
as my mother suggests. Lately,
I sit by the window watching
grackles perched on power lines.
They're the only birds on my block.
An acupuncturist told me once
it weakens the eyes to stare at birds.
Look for green meadows, he said.

Where I live now there are no meadows,
only rows of gray live-oaks
with profuse and dense leaves.
Without my glasses, they're dark,
monolithic shapes, looming mysteries.

Eight years old, I squinted
through two entire terms in Malta.
After Brother Martin turned off the lights,
what I saw outside the window each night
must have really been white doves
circling the steeples of San Giuseppi,
not the angels I believed they were.
I couldn't see the stars
that must have been out there.

. . .

Where I live now there are no stars,
the night yellow with city lights,
a sulphur dome separating this place
and that clarity we long for.
Is vision a kind of desire,
the need to see things we want
and places we'd rather be?
I used to think near-sightedness
was every child's natural affliction,
inevitable like leaving home.

Still each night I prayed
for the angels over San Giuseppi
to fly closer to my window,
and offer to take me home.

Marilyn Chin

Phil Toy

Marilyn Chin majored in ancient Chinese literature at the University of Massachusetts at Amherst and received her M.F.A. in poetry from The Iowa workshop in 1981. Chin was born in Hong Kong and raised in Portland, Oregon. She is the author of *Dwarf Bamboo* (Greenfield Review Press, 1987), which was nominated for the Bay Area Book Reviewers Award. Currently, she is on the faculty of the M.F.A. program at San Diego State University, and her recent poems have appeared in *The Iowa Review, Ploughshares, The Kenyon Review,* and *Parnassus,* as well as *The Norton Introduction to Poetry.* She is the recipient of a Stegner Fellowship, a National Endowment for the Arts Writing Fellowship, and a Mary Roberts Rinehart award. She has held residences at Yaddo, the MacDowell Colony, Centrum, Virginia Center for the Creative Arts, and the Djerassi Foundation. She has just completed her second book of poems, *The Phoenix Gone, The Terrace Empty.*

Exile's Letter *(Or: An Essay on Assimilation)*

from a distant cousin, circa 1964

We are in Louisiana now
planting soy for an aristocrat
with a French surname,
I think, Prevert; and no,
he's not what his name suggests,
but rather, a stoic, truthful man,
a professed de Gaulian
devoted to Mother France
and understands, so he says,
the plight of the races.
Too bad that his wife, mad
and dying of cancer,
has offered him no children,
an unjust retribution
for a man so sure of his creed.
One cool summer evening,
and the field alight with flies,
she came to us, whispering
"There were dogs here
who vanished in the deep of the night,
prized setters and pointers,
well-groomed and with papers.
I don't believe you have erred
and have eaten ours as your own."
Grandmother touched her arm.
"Let us speak the truth, Madame,
it was *your* dogs, remember,
who crossed the fence,
who delighted in our cabbage."
The woman nodded and cried,
"Oh my little children,"
then, drove off into the sunset
in her station wagon filled

with seed for fodder.
"The dying are not unwise,
even the most dessicated cactus
issues a flower before death."
Grandmother said this, gazing
at the vast, cultivated wasteland.
Life goes on, Mei Ling,
Even I've bloomed lovelier, I think,
resembling you a little,
but rounder where profitable.
And behind that briared fence
the boys are watching, even now,
the white boys.

Repulse Bay

Hong Kong, Summer 1980

1

Washed ashore
At Repulse Bay
Creatures that outgrew their shells—
I saw a mussel hang
On a shell's hinge: the sun
Turned its left side brown
What remained tarried
Around the lips
Like a human tongue
Unfit for speech

Suddenly, the sea
Sweeps it up, with
A stub-necked bottle, bits of feces and the news
Printed in red and black
Bilingual editions for the Colonialists
And two-bit Japanese tourists
Seeking thrills

2

Back to Kowloon, in Granny's
One room apartment, her laundry waves
On her sun-filled balcony—
I recognize some of mine: blue jeans, bright T's
A black lace bra on a hook . . .
Two stories below, an old hawker
Selling abalone on a stick, chicken asses
Pig ears, tripe of all species burnt pink—
Looks up, shakes his fist

3

The rain over Hong Kong falls
Over all of us, Li Ching, though
This postcard will tell you nothing
About the country I have lost

Overhead, a building blinks
Of Rolex, Omega and yet
Another brand that ticks

4

Last night, drunk out of my mind
I promised everybody visas and a good time
(should they make it to America)
Autumn is here now, though
There are no rustling New England leaves
Or Oregon grapes tugging the vines

5

How the sun shines through the monsoon brightly
On the small men selling viscera
On the dead and swimming creatures of the sea

American Rain

for Vin Xu, half Chinese, all Vietnamese

I.

To our mother, maimed
twenty years ago by Japanese
shrapnel, and father
who has willed his skull
to the vault of the sky,
his flesh to the grey loess,
his blood to the sea,
I pledge that we will be safe
in our new country
and the Peng-bird will shit
now on another man's rooftop,
and ours, neither thatch nor bamboo,
will endure
another severe winter . . .

II.

In Hanoi, our cousin Vin Xu blooms beautifully—
a lily on the marl of the dead;
and across the Ben Hai River,
over the coconut palms, the arroyos,
500 meters beyond the Hero's Cloud Pass,
over the five peaks of marble,
his wife, Mya, carries
a basket of manioc on her head; carries
her small crippled child on her back; carries
her small dead child in her arms.

III.

American thunders, bombers' rain,
my brother with a blue chest of stars
unfolded a map under their native sky—
tiny flags where the victories were;
deaths were gold stars.

"They don't look like us, they're
smaller, darker, quick as flies."
He rocks as his half-white child
on his lap as he says this; its lips
pursed into a smile.

On our porch in Seaside Oregon
the sun sets in its own scarlet reflection,
joggers on the boardwalk turn, wave,
unvexed by the drizzle.
This hour in the life of the sea,

what shall I do this hour?
Wash my long hair, let it dry
under the sun; rest my head
against my arms' hard cradle
as the wind blows the black clouds over?

When I gaze beyond my elbow
what can I see: stars
which are distant, unclear,
pines dwarfed as palmettos, bent
by the sea.

And where dark green conifers
meet the sky, one dinghy
at the edge of vision—
a young man lingers on the deck, soaks in
the last of the sun.

Is there a boat that doesn't veer towards heaven?
Is there a heaven that doesn't yearn for its boats?

IV.

In the beginning was the unblinking eye
The mouth which never ceased moving
The soft, swollen belly
Shiny as a hall of mirrors
My husband holds it by the tail
How it wags and flickers
How it is best marinated
Steamed and scallioned to my delight

I sit on the crag, the wind
Fingers through my wet hair
I watch my son and his friends dive
Off the promontory, their jackknives
unfolding, the air
Seizing them for moments
Clean entrances, no splash
Their small heads surface

V.

Nam
Ngai
Binh
Phu
Phan
Thiet
Southward, one
decoy, another,
oleander, cattail
float under them.
A sky of black birds—perhaps
egret, perhaps geese, a foreboding
of jets—wing over them.
Vin Xu questions the clouds;
Mya nags the wind:

with each stone that falls, each branch that snaps,
how many of us will arrive
at the ports of America where
large ships from Brazil, Africa
unload paradise
fruit, sugar, tea. No one
in this ocean can understand
another's war. The machines
of war are amphibious.
The half-men are cunning, though
they are blind in one eye, they can drive
with one arm.
Vietnam,
forget your bamboo palaces,
your grass fortresses, your bog-moats.

VI.

Her body sways all the night long
Her mind still tugging on the Ben Hai River
Her belly swells
Not with food but with hunger
There is no world she does not fear
There is no world without fear

Barbarian Suite

for David Wong Louie

1

The Ming will be over to make way for the Ch'ing.
The Ch'ing will be over to make way for eternity.
The East is red and the sun is rising.
All bleeds into the ocean in the Califia west.
My loss is your loss, a dialect here, a memory there—
if my left hand is dying will my right hand cut it off?
We shall all be vestigial organs, the gift of democracy.
The pale faces, the wan conformity,
the price we pay for comfort is our mother tongue.

2

China is an ocean away, our grandmother beaconing
with too many children, too many mouths to feed.
We can no longer dress her and improve her accent.
We can no longer toil in her restaurant "Double Happiness,"
    oiling woks, peeling shrimp.
She is the bridge—and we've broken her back with our weight.
We study Western philosophy and explore our raison d'être.
All is well in the suburbs when we are in love with poetry.

3

What did ya think, the emperor will come to your grave?
To tell ya all is groovy in the hinterlands?
What did ya think? Life's that honky-dory?
What did ya expect, old peasant, old fool,
one day out of the woods and the dirt will eject
    from your nostrils?
Even dung-heaps will turn fragrant with a thorough cleansing?

4

Orchids doth not bloom, baby, they cry, they explode.
Meanwhile our anger gets muted in their facial beauty—
AmerAsia so harmonious under a canopy of stars.
The pram of a new nation, the winds rock it gently.
Truth has no face, we make it wear ours.
You walk on the beach with your beautiful son Julian.
We dare to eat peaches and discuss the classics.

5

One day they came to me, my dead ancestors.
They whispered *sse-sse-sse,* homophonous with "death."
I was under the covers with my barbarian boyfriend.
blowing smokerings, talking jazz—"Posterity"
is yet another "compromising position,"
    an addenda to the Kama Sutra.
I was playing Goddess/Dominatress
and kept a piece of his ear as offering.

6

Cauldron full, cauldron empty.
The duck dangling in the window is the last vestige
of our sizzling suzerainty.
They believed in order, which meant victory over oblivion.
They believed in the restaurant called "Double Happiness."
Where all the partners were brothers, all the sisters wore brocade.
The cash-register rang its daily prayer wheels
for the dying and the saved.

Eric Chock

Ghislaine Dubois

Eric Chock was born in 1950. He received his B.A.
from the University of Pennsylvania and his M.A. from the
University of Hawaii. He serves as Poet and Program Co-
ordinator for the Hawaii Poets in the Schools program in
Honolulu. His first book, *Last Days Here,* was published by
the Bamboo Ridge Press in 1990.

Working Construction

In those days, I couldn't tell if I was strong.
But I survived our 60's style
rites of passage, every night till 2:00 a.m.
the sweet carcinogenic blend of Marlboros and pot,
the music and the bitter lick of alcohol
hardening our tongues for the coming years
of manhood, a still-soft first kiss
fading in a hotel lagoon.
And by dawn, a quick eggs and juice
and I'd shoot down to the E.E. Black job yard
to huddle in the back of a big green pickup
listening to Manuel steam our coffee
with stories of how many pregnant girls in P.I.
chased this manong clear out of his country,
and how many here are trying to send him back,
and him only laughing as we bounced our asses
down new stretches of freeway,
steel toes and dirt-stiff jeans and t-shirts
shivering in the first-light blues of Honolulu.
I was just a drop-out from college;
some of these guys were actually killers, con artists,
all kinds of thieves, ready to rip off
any small piece of reality.

For some, like Manuel, reality was talking girls
all day, even while waist-deep in a watercress patch
scooping out the foundations for the Waiau overpass,
a litany of tits, bilots, and erections
chanting us through whole mornings of mud.
As if for emphasis, he'd grab a big crayfish
off my shovel, rip off its mini-lobster tail,
and with a quick swish in a clean spot of water
down the delicacy with a whiskery grin,

tossing the waving claws and pointy nose
over his shoulders to the sky.

For Masa, who asked me to join his carpenters' union
to learn a skill, reality was slipping on his way
to the bathtubs he was installing,
and then falling three stories inside
the hollow new wing of Queen's Hospital.
He landed down where a sparse field
of steel re-bars was still standing 2 feet tall
out from the concrete foundation, waiting
for their next layer. He flew down
and got one through the wing,
missing his lung and heart, and months later
grinned and lifted his white t-shirt
to show me his scars.

There was the one I was afraid of,
I never knew his name, he was a Hawaiian
who had murdered his unfaithful wife.
Behind his black shades he must have
re-lived his pain, as he sat
alone in a heavy protective cage all day
shifting the gears of the tall crane
that swung the huge bucket, sloppy with concrete,
in a heavy arc up to the highest floors.

It was Big Charlie and me up there,
kids with a gigantic metal ice cream cone
filled with a quarter ton of grey mush,
him chuting it into the 8″ forms
while I stuffed it down before it stiffened,
backstepping in rhythmic strokes
7 stories in the air, with no railings,
no handholds, nothing but my shovel
keeping me balanced up there,
so lost in my confidence

and the steady flow of the pour, that in mid-stroke
I backed right off the end of the wall.

On one foot I tilted, shovel releasing,
the other foot lifting like a crane dying
in a tai chi pose, and Charlie reached around
and grabbed my arm and squeezed me back,
and for once I was glad to be skinny.
Take it easy, he said, 3 of the few words
he ever spoke to me.

Charlie took it easy.
Everyone knew how he primed himself each day.
Once I saw him take his rigs, jab himself,
and then jam 7 hours straight
on a jackhammer, alone, cracking
old walls to dust, covering himself
with powder till he glowed
like the angels that blasted him
through his brief eternity.
Lunchtimes, in the parking lot,
safe and resting in the octopus roots of a banyan tree
he was dealing the stuff, heroin;
and all I could think was, he saved me.

The last job site that year was in Hell
or maybe Purgatory, I don't know which
is a flat, salty, crushed-coral plain in Ewa
where no trees, no wind, no sound exist,
except for the rippling 90 degree heat
that can pulse the sweat from your face.

It was a graveyard for used forms
flaking the concrete from their last wall,
all sizes of iron scaffolding, their heavy
H-frames rubbing off some of your palms,
and 4 by 8 plywood warping their last layers

as they were washed and stacked
for their next incarnation.

We were like boys gathering our Tinkertoys,
counting up how many we had of each piece,
although, in reality, we didn't care
cause we never got to construct our own fantasies.
And it was so hot we worked for 30 minutes,
then took breaks in makeshift shade,
sucking water from a cooler.
One guy always went for long shits
in the SANITOI, a risky place
to open a zipper with dozens of scorpions
keeping time on the walls.
One day somebody peeked in,
found him giving himself a dirty handjob,
desperate for a little ecstasy in the dim,
stinking closet of his little heaven.

Poem for George Helm:
Aloha Week 1980

I was in love with the word "aloha"
Even though I heard it over and over
I let the syllables ring in my ears
and I believed the king with outstretched hand
was welcoming everyone who wanted to live here
And I ignored the spear in his left hand
believing instead my fellow humans
and their love for these islands in the world
which allow us to rest from the currents
and moods of that vast ocean from which we all came
But George Helm's body is back in that ocean
I want to believe in the greatness of his spirit
that he still feels the meaning of that word
which is getting so hard to say.

I thought there was hope for the word "aloha"
I believed when they said there are ways
in this modern technological world Oahu alone
could hold a million people
And we would become the Great Crossroads of the Pacific
if we used our native aloha spirit
our friendly wahines and our ancient hulas
They showed us our enormous potential
and we learned to love it
like a man who loves some thing in gold or silver
But these islands are made of lava and trees and sand
A man learns to swim with the ocean
and when he's tired he begins to search
for what he loves, for what will sustain him
George Helm is lost at sea
The bombing practice continues on Kahoolawe
I want to believe in what he was seeking

I want to believe that he is still swimming
toward that aina for which he feels
that word which is so hard to say

I want to believe in the word
But Brother George doesn't say it
He doesn't sing it in his smooth falsetto
in the melodies of aloha aina
There is no chance of seeing him walk up to the stage
pick up his guitar and smile the word at you across the room
The tourists, they twist their malihini tongues
The tour guides mount it with smog-filled lungs
Politicians keep taking it out, dusting off the carcass
of a once-proud 3 syllable guaranteed vote-getter
You find its ghosts on dump trucks, magazines
airplanes, rent-a-cars
anywhere they want the dollar
They can sell you anything with aloha and a smile
even pineapples that they brought here from
(you guessed it) America!
They'll sell you too, servants of the USA
And if you don't believe they have the nerve
think of the ocean
They put up signs as close as they dare
And when his spirit comes back to land
the first thing he'll see is a big sign with that word
painted on, carved in, flashing with electricity
That word, so hard to say

I was going to believe that word
I was going to believe all those corporations
that seemed to spring up like mushrooms after a light
rain
I was going to believe when they divided up
the home-land of a living people
and called it real estate, or 50th state
or, Aloha State
I was going to believe we would still be able

to go up to the mountains, out to the country beaches
So many trying to swim in the waves
legs kicking, arms paddling like the arms
of George Helm stroking towards a familiar beach
which he respected and belonged to by birth
for which he felt something no word can express
except for that word which is hard to say
unless we all live it

I want to live the word "aloha"
But the body of George Helm is lost at sea
the practice continues on Kahoolawe
the buildings follow the roads
the roads carry thousands of cars filled with people
following their dreams of Hawaii or Paradise
to Waikiki where girls sell their hips
singers sell their voices
the island which has been sold is lit up all night
while the king with outstretched hand
has forgotten how to use his spear
George Helm is dead
and that word
it rings in my ears every day
I want us to live the word "aloha"
but it's so hard just to say

The Bait

Saturday mornings, before
my weekly chores,
I used to sneak out of the house
and across the street,
grabbing the first grasshopper
waking in the damp California grass
along the stream.
Carefully hiding a silver hook
beneath its green wings,
I'd float it out
across the gentle ripples
towards the end of its life.
Just like that.
I'd give it the hook
and let it ride.
All I ever expected for it
was that big-mouth bass
awaiting its arrival.
I didn't think
that I was giving up one life
to get another,
that even childhood
was full of sacrifice.
I'd just take the bright green thing,
pluck it off its only stalk,
and give it away as if
it were mine to give.
I knew someone out there
would be fooled,
that someone would accept
the precious gift.
So I just sent it along
with a plea of a prayer,

hoping it would spread its wings this time
and fly across that wet glass sky,
no concern for what inspired
its life, or mine,
only instinct guiding pain
towards the other side.

Chitra Banerjee Divakaruni

Dhruva Banerjee

Chitra Banerjee Divakaruni, born in 1956 and origi-
nally from India, teaches creative writing at Foothill Col-
lege, California, where she is a director for the annual
national Creative Writing Conference. Her work has ap-
peared in magazines such as *Calyx, Chelsea, The Beloit Poetry
Journal, Colorado Review, Indiana Review,* and *The Threepenny
Review.* She has published three books of poems: *Dark Like
the River* (Writers Workshop, India, 1987), *The Reason for
Nasturtiums* (Berkeley Poets Press, 1990), and *Black Candle*
(Calyx Books, 1991). She is also the editor of an upcoming
anthology of multicultural writing, *Multitude,* to be re-
leased by McGraw-Hill in 1992. Her awards include a
Santa Clara Arts Council Award, Barbara Deming Memo-
rial Award, Cecil Hackney Literary Award, and an Editor's
Choice Award from the *Cream City Review,* among others.

Childhood

It was a place where apples sprouted teeth,
the wild duck father shot in the Fall
hung neck down in its purple pimpled skin.
A place where stacked blocks of dark
topped at the wrong password, where
all the wooden arrows you aimed
quivering and comet-tailed at enormous suns
reappeared flecked with red. And the dreams—
were they always of crows with obsidian beaks,
palmyra trees that turned to tongues or wounds,
and under that twisted judas vine
on your way each day to the yellow school bus
the hunchbacked beggar woman with iron hair
and how you knew you couldn't say no
if she opened the bloated sack of her body
and invited you in.

Outside Pisa

Above the Boca del Arno the sky
bleeds its last red. The sea gives up
its colors to the dark. On the barren shore
we stand trying to hold hands,
to smile like lovers. The fishermen
have left their nets and poles, black and jagged
against the night's coming. Nothing
left for us to say. Smell of salt
and death, older than this broken harbor, older
than the white tower
this morning by the cathedral

After all the pictures, how small it seemed,
how fragile in its leaning. Dark slits of stairs,
the sooty upturned spiral, the holding on,
walls damp and slippery to the palm,
surface-scratched with names and hopes:
*Lorenzo e Rosa, Pietro, Clementina, Sally
loves Bill.* And when we came out
into the hot light, all around us
the breathless rainbow sheen of pigeon wings,
couples kissing, mouth to moist
rose-mouth. This same death-smell.
The floor tilted away
from my feet. No railings, just
the adrenalin rush of white edge
into nothing. You were taking pictures. I
kept my face turned away. In case
you saw my eyes, my longing to jump.

When the doctor said
I couldn't have children, I sensed
the stiffening in your bones. We never
spoke of it. Deep
bell-sounds from the baptistry
where they say Galileo discovered
the centripetal motion of this world,
the headlong, wheeling planets held
arc upon arc, calm and enormous,
without accident.
Now I let go your stranger's hand,
the unfamiliar callus on your thumb.
We are suspended as dust
in this dark river air, floating
away from each other, from the other shore
where we cannot be,
its gleam of fairy lights
that we would die for.

Indigo

Bengal, 1779–1859

The fields flame with it, endless, blue
as cobra poison. It has entered
our blood and pulses
up our veins like night. There is
no other color. The planter's whip
splits open the flesh of our faces,
a blue liquid light trickles
through the fingers. Blue dyes the lungs
when we breathe. Only the obstinate eyes

refuse to forget where once the rice
parted the earth's moist skin
and pushed up reed by reed,
green, then rippled gold
like the Arhiyal's waves. Stitched
into our eyelids, the broken dark,
the torches of the planter's men,
fire walling like a tidal wave that
flattened the ripe grain with a smell
like charred flesh, broke
on our huts. And the wind
screaming in the voices of women
dragged to the plantation,
feet, hair, torn breasts.

In the worksheds, we dip our hands,
their violent forever blue,
in the dye, pack it
in great embossed chests
for the East India Company.
Our ankles gleam thin blue
from the chains. After that night

many of the women killed
themselves. Drowning
was the easiest.
Sometimes the Arhiyal gave us back
the naked, bloated bodies, the faces
eaten by fish. We hold on
to red, the color
of their saris, the marriage mark
on their foreheads,
we hold it carefully inside
our blue skulls, like a man
in the cold *Paush* night
holds in his cupped palms
a spark, its welcome scorch,
feeds it his foggy breath
till he can set it down
in the right place,
to blaze up and burst
like the hot heart of a star
over the whole horizon,
a burning so beautiful you want it
to never end.

Note: Indigo planting was forced on the farmers of Bengal, India, by the British, who exported it as a cash crop for almost a hundred years until the peasant uprising of 1860, when the plantations were destroyed.

The Brides Come to Yuba City

The sky is hot and yellow, filled
with blue screaming birds. The train
heaved us from its belly
and vanished in shrill smoke.
Now only the tracks
gleam dull in the heavy air,
a ladder to eternity, each receding rung
cleaved from our husbands' ribs.
Mica-flecked, the platform
dazzles, burns up through thin
chappal soles, lurches
like the ship's dark hold,
blurred month of nights, smell of vomit,
a porthole like the bleached iris
of a giant unseeing eye.

Red-veiled, we lean into each other,
press damp palms, try
broken smiles. The man
who met us at the ship whistles
a restless *Angrezi* tune
and scans the fields. Behind us,
the black wedding trunks, sharp-edged,
shiny, stenciled with strange men-names
our bodies do not fit into:
Mrs. Baldev Fohl, Mrs. Kanwal Bains.
Inside, folded like wings,
bright *salwar kameezes* scented
with sandalwood. For the men,
kurtas and thin white gauze
to wrap their uncut hair.
Laddus from Jullundhar, sugar-crusted,
six kinds of lentils, a small bag

of *bajra* flour. Labeled in our mothers'
hesitant hands, pickled mango and lime,
packets of seeds—*methi, karela, saag*—
to burst from this new soil
like green stars.

He gives a shout, waves
at the men, their slow
uneven approach. We crease our eyes
through the veils' red film,
cannot breathe. Thirty years
since we saw them. Or never,
like Harvinder, married last year
at Hoshiarpur to her husband's photo,
which she clutches tight to her
to stop the shaking. He is fifty-two,
she sixteen. Tonight—like us all—
she will open her legs to him.

The platform is endless-wide.
The men walk and walk
without advancing. Their lined,
wavering mouths, their
eyes like drowning lights.
We cannot recognize a single face.

Note: Yuba City in northern California was settled largely by Indian railroad workers around the 1900s.
Due to immigration restrictions, many of them were unable to bring their families over—or, in the
case of single men, go back to get married—until the 1940s.

Yuba City School

From the black trunk I shake out
my one American skirt, blue serge
that smells of mothballs. Again today
Neeraj came crying from school. All week
the teacher has made him sit
in the last row, next to the fat boy
who drools and mumbles,
picks at the spotted milk-blue
skin of his face, but knows
to pinch, sudden-sharp,
when she is not looking.

The books are full of black curves,
dots like the eggs the boll-weevil lays
each monsoon in furniture-cracks
in Ludhiana. Far up in front
the teacher makes word-sounds
Neeraj does not know. They float
from her mouth-cave, he says,
in discs, each a different color.

Candy-pink for the girls
in their lace dresses, marching
shiny shoes. Silk-yellow
for the boys beside them,
crisp blond hair, hands raised
in all the right answers. Behind them
the Mexicans, whose older brothers,
he tells me, carry knives,
whose catcalls and whizzing rubber bands
clash, mid-air, with the teacher's
voice, its sharp purple edge.
For him, the words are
a muddy red, flying low and heavy,
and always the one he has learned to understand:
idiot, idiot, idiot.

I heat the iron over the stove. Outside
evening blurs the shivering
in the eucalyptus. Neeraj's shadow
disappears into the hole
he is hollowing all afternoon.
The earth, he knows, is round, and if
one can tunnel all the way through,
he will end up in Punjab,
in his grandfather's mango orchard,
his grandmother's songs lighting
on his head, the old words
glowing like summer fireflies.

In the playground, Neeraj says,
invisible hands snatch at his uncut hair,
unseen feet trip him from behind,
and when he turns, ghost laughter
all around his bleeding knees.
He bites down on his lip
to keep in the crying. They are
waiting for him to open his mouth,
so they can steal his voice.

I test the iron with little drops of water
that sizzle and die. Press down
on the wrinkled cloth. The room fills
with a smell like singed flesh.
Tomorrow in my blue skirt I will go
to see the teacher, my tongue
stiff and swollen
in my unwilling mouth, my few
English phrases. She will pluck them
from me, nail shut my lips. My son
will keep sitting in the last row
among the red words that drink his voice.

Note: The boy in the poem is a Sikh immigrant, whose religion forbids the cutting of his hair.

Alfred Encarnacion

Alfred Encarnacion was born in Philadelphia in 1958, the product of a biracial marriage: Filipino father, American mother. He presently teaches at Temple University, where he completed his B.A. in English (1980) and M.A. in creative writing (1990). His chapbook, *At Winter's End*, appeared in 1986 with Limbo Press. His poems have appeared in *Indiana Review, Sabal Palm Review,* and *Wind,* and his work has been republished in the *Anthology of Magazine Verse* and *Yearbook of American Poetry.* He has received awards from the Indiana Writers Conference and the Academy of American Poets. His project is "to articulate aspects of Filipino-American experience previously ignored or censored in the historical context of our culture."

Threading the Miles

In Memory of Carlos Bulosan, 1911–1956

I move to the window
that's filled with wet light.

I thread a small needle and
set to work, noting how rain
falls so easily like sewing a rip

in the breast of this shirt, not
taking it off, though I'm risking

bad luck. I should be writing
a poem about Carlos Bulosan,
his exile in America:

how he faced the rain, the
violence, how he made *adobo*

with scrap meat from garbage,
how he bummed miles to find work,
dreaming of the family he'd left

on Luzon. What stitches our dreams
through our bodies like threads

through cloth? Each dream,
each stitch, a solitary act,
a lonely art. While I sew,

a woman walks by in the rain
outside—old, slow, oblivious

as stone. Vietnamese, maybe
Cambodian. Dressed like the poor
in such jarring garments: orange

and purple colliding with green.
She carries a Pepsi, a wet bag

from Wendy's and no umbrella.
She walks in a daze, yet
with deep resignation. I know

how some of us move by rote,
as if the light of our minds hovered

in other places. I imagine paddies,
jungles, thunderous plateaus
across the sea, ominous journeys

undertaken in private when parts
of our lives wash away or collapse

around us, leaving chasms and
no direction but the long road
into darkness. The tear

in the cloth disappears. I pull
the thread tight, as though

stitching my heart, sew in the knot.
When I look out the window
the old woman has vanished, lost

in the rainy afternoon haze. Somehow
I'm stricken, thinking of miles

so cruel they boggle the mind.
Wait. Come back. Share with us. . . .
And Bulosan tramps down a highway

through yellow fog in the California
rain, on his way to pick fruit

in the Yakima Valley. 1936.
The year of pariah: Pinoys gunned down
in the streets of white towns.

Fog starting to lift, clean sun
burning through. . . . This young man—

mid-twenties, beautifully alone,
his wet clothes ragged,
his boots caked with red mud—

slips a flat, amber bottle
out of his pocket, takes

a deep swig, takes another.
The road stretches forward
as from a spool of black thread,

disappears through the eye
of a needle.

Bulosan Listens to
a Recording of
Robert Johnson

You sing a hard blues,
black man. You too have been driven:
a tumbleweed in strong wind.
I close my eyes, your voice rolls
out of the delta, sliding
over flashy chords
that clang like railroad tracks.

Gotta keep movin'
Gotta keep movin'
Hellhound on my trail

One summer
I worked the *wash-lye*
section of a cannery up north,
scrubbed schools of headless fish,
breathed ammonia fumes so fierce
I almost floated off
like the arm of a friend,
chopped clean at the elbow
by a cutter's machine.

Gotta keep movin'
Gotta keep movin'

We are the blue men, *Cabayan,*
our pockets empty of promise.
Mississippi, California—
bad luck conspires against us,
cheap wine stings in our veins.
We reel, drunk and bitter,

under the white, legal sun.
Robert Johnson/Carlos Bulosan—
our names so different,
our song the same.

Seattle, Autumn, 1933

Once more the leaves
fall, flecked with messages
from the dead. Their spiraling
descent signaturing winter:
the immigrants tremble, terrified
like all vagrants of the cold,
the cruel language of snow,
of wind policing this city.
These days I note a firm hesitation
before I can write, as before
I awake I seem to hold onto
the last thread of sleep
as it's pulled into light
through the blue eye of morning.
Now it's late afternoon.
Soon the moon will rise
from the sea's gnarled mist,
a yellow beacon. I try to hide
my shame in measures of song
as I witness the plight
of lives squandered in dance halls,
in gambling houses . . . vats of
bootleg whiskey fermenting . . .
dens filled with secret opium
dreams . . . and Chinatown Roses,
their cash-only smiles, shimmer
at windows, grimy with sin.
But I'm torn by men who wander
these streets like tattered ghosts,
women huddled in shadows,
stirring pots of thin soup,
and that child who knelt
one night in a lot,

strangely lit by a bonfire,
who feasted on nothing
but dark, scraggly leaves
and smiled as she hymned
to Our Lady of Flames . . .
How weather this grief
that numbs into silence?
How may my pen provoke
beauty, not anger?
Nothing inside me feels
tempted to sing. Unless
grievance is song. The
fierce scrape of dead leaf
against leaf, music.

Eugene Gloria

Kristen Lindquist

Eugene Gloria was born in Manila, Philippines, in 1957 and moved with his family to San Francisco in 1966. He received his B.A. from San Francisco State University, his M.A. from Miami University in Ohio, and his M.F.A. from the University of Oregon. His poems have appeared in *Parnassus, Blue Mesa Review, Quarry West,* and *Asian America,* among others.

In Language

for K.L.

After we make love, I teach you
words I'm slowly forgetting: names
for hands, breast, hair and river.
And in the telling, I find myself
astonished, recalling the music
in my grandmother's words before
she left this world—words you
don't forget, like a mandate
from heaven. She said: It's in
the act of cleansing that we kill
the spirit—ourselves,
every culture's worst enemy
is its own people.

And so I teach you, to remind
myself what it means when I say:
hali ka dito, come here, tell me
the names for ocean, stars, river,
and sun—and you tell me what you
remember from the moments
in which the telling arose; you say—
hair instead of river; you say breasts,
instead of hands, you say
cock and cunt
instead of moon, sea, and stars.

Milkfish

You feed us milkfish stew
and long grain rice, make us eat
blood soup with chili peppers,
and frown at us when we lose our appetite.
I remember when I was young and you
told me of that monsoon: the Japanese occupation—
stories of a time before you met my father,
when you learned the language
of an occupied city in order to feed your family.
You were the pretty one at seventeen,
your skin, white as milkfish.
The pretty ones, you said,
were always given more food—
the Japanese soldiers, sentried above
the loft where you worked dropped
sweet yams and you caught them
by the billow of your skirt.
I remember you in sepia-brown photographs
of a *mestiza* who equated liberation
with Hershey bars and beige nylons
from American GIs—and the season of the monsoon,
as dark as hunger, was not about suffering
but what you knew of beauty.

The Whisper

In the ripest days of August, sunflowers
droop their heavy heads as if listening.
It was from such a posture
that my Lolo Panta learned those words
he mumbled over fetishes,
over tonics he concocted, over the ache
of muscles and high fevers,
over neatly folded clothes he kept
in a dresser drawers rank
with the smell of church candles and wood.
At his last hour, Lolo Panta lay
longing for his children, a white handkerchief
folded in a band around his throat
like Father Tiodoro's collar,
concealing the hole round as a communion host.
Mornings when his house on the Abenida
was empty except for his dog,
Lolo Panta would sneak a Salem menthol
and drag a rich lungful through the hole,
exhaling his forbidden pleasure
with eyes clinched shut.
                              Years after my Lolo died,
my mother told me with indifference
about duendes: sprites and demons
born from the belly of the Pasig River.
Their spirits live through *mangkukulams,*
those who hold life on the blink of an eye,
or a curse—like the Blessed Virgin
of Guadalupe trampling the heads of snakes.
My Lolo healed victims of spells
by whispering the language of duendes
over his amulets: small pieces of wood carved
with the sign of the cross. He burned them,

waiting for the the evil spirit's face
to appear in the screen of white smoke.
He'd melt candles for expectant mothers
and with the wax determine the sex of the child.
                              My mother was my Lolo's
third child born between a sister who died at birth,
and a brother who died in his second summer.

She inherited by virtue of surviving
the power to heal with touch,
the smooth glide of hands
against skin and sore limbs,
the hard grind of her open palms,
fingers working in saliva or the strong
aroma of Vicks VapoRub.
                              When the mounds of earth
where duendes lived were leveled by the growth
of buildings and new houses, my mother found
a job at Traveler's Life answering phones.
The language of the village withered inside her
when she took up the voice of American movies,
and the spirits of the siblings she was born between
hid away beneath the river.
                              In his final hour,
inside the room where he once parcelled
powdered cures in small brown envelopes,
Lolo Panta bent in the sunburnt heat and whispered
the words to his dog sitting beside him.
Later the dog trotted away sniffing at the mounds
behind my Lolo's house, and my mother
began her long workday as usual.

Vince Gotera

Vince Gotera

Vince Gotera was born in San Francisco in June 1952,
but lived for some years as a child in the Philippines. He is
an Assistant Professor of English at Humboldt State Uni-
versity, where he teaches creative writing and American
ethnic literature. He received his Ph.D. and M.F.A. from
Indiana University, but he has studied as well at Stanford,
San Francisco State, and City College of San Francisco.
Gotera has finished his book of poems, *Pacific Crossing*. His
book of criticism, *Radical Visions: Poetry by Vietnam Veterans,*
is forthcoming from the University of Georgia Press.
His poems have appeared in *Caliban, Kenyon Review, ART/
LIFE, Seattle Review, Indiana Review,* and other literary jour-
nals. He has won the Academy of American Poets Prize,
the Felix Pollak Poetry Prize at the University of Wiscon-
sin, and the Mary Roberts Rinehart Award in Poetry. He
is poetry editor of *Asian America,* a journal of arts and
culture published by the University of California at Santa
Barbara.

Dance of the Letters

My father, in a 1956 gray suit,
had the jungle in his tie,
a macaw on Kelly green.
But today is Saturday, no briefs
to prepare, and he's in a T-shirt.

I sit on his lap with my *ABC*
Golden Book, and he orders the letters
to dance. The *A* prancing red
as an apple, the *E* a lumbering elephant,
the *C* chased by the *D* while the sly *F*

is snickering in his russet fur coat.
My mother says my breakthrough
was the *M* somersaulting into a *W.*
Not a mouse transformed into a wallaby
at all, but sounds that we can see.

Later, my father trots me out
to the living room like a trained *Z.*
Not yet four, I read newspaper headlines
out loud for Tito Juanito and Tita Naty
or for anyone who drops in.

Six years later, I am that boy
in a black Giants cap, intertwining orange
letters *S* and *F,* carrying my father's
forgotten lunch to the catacombs
of the UCSF Medical Center,
and I love the hallway cool before the swirling,
heat from the Print Shop door.
In his inky apron, my father smiles,
but his eyes are tired. The night before,
I pulled the pillow over my head, while he

argued with my mother
till two a.m. about that old double bind:
a rule to keep American citizens from
practicing law in the Philippines.
His University of Manila

law degree made useless.
But California's just as bad.
"You can't work in your goddamn
profession stateside either!" he shouts.
"Some land of opportunity."

There in the shimmer of the Print Shop, I can't
understand his bitterness. I savor
the staccato sounds. He leans
into the noise of huge machines, putting
vowels and consonants into neat stacks.

Gambling

In the 50s, we drove each month to my uncle's house.
Springing from the car, Papa would joke with him,
"The American Dream, ha, *Kumpadre?* No sleep
till Monday." Then they'd play mah jongg non-stop
and we cousins, sleeping under whispering
gauze, dreamed of Arabian nights, Sinbad,

genies with palaces nestled in their palms.
Those Saturday and Sunday mornings, the kids would build
castles with mah-jongg tiles piled up in walls
of many colors, which my cousin Levy
would demolish with a sweep of his hand.
We were mystified by cries of *"Kang!*

Mah jongg! Pong!" We didn't yet have dreams
of horses named *Flip Side* or *Pearl of the Orient.*
Jai-alai and cockfights—just games.
Not yet insomniac rounds of Keno, dollar
slots or poker. We hadn't yet entered
that airy mansion *Long Shot* built from clouds.

How could we have predicted the chill of adrenalin
from snake-eyes? Up against the wall, crapped out.
Papa's weekend trips to Reno were
a calculus of chance. Any day now,
Lady Luck would wave her *Ninang's* wand
in our direction. You never know. What's that?

Romantic, you say? I want to tell you mah jongg
is real. Hard and cruel as the Napa asylum
where my childhood friend stares into
oblivion. My *kumpadre,* José Manalo.
He can't escape it, lives it over and over.

How he had scrimped on lunches to join the "Empress
of China Tour" bound for Reno. From the bus,
he and his partners flipped off the old-timers
hanging out on Kearny. Yeah, they were going
big time, no more tonk for 10 and 20.
Jose saw Chinese ideographs in Harrah's
Oriental Room and copied them off the walls

onto Keno cards. In his mind, they said
long life, wealth, or *dreams come true.*
On his last try, 10 minutes before
the bus was scheduled to leave, he matched 9
spots—50 grand. *Manalo: a winner.*
He knew he had to claim the prize before

the next game, 5 minutes at most. But *balato,*
the Filipino custom of spreading your luck,
meant at least a hundred bucks in each
of his buddies' pockets. So he strolled
with his friends to the bus, then said
he'd forgotten his coat. As the bus revved up,

he sprinted back into Harrah's
where the Keno boss waved him away.
"I'm sorry, buddy, you know you've got to collect
before a new game begins," and he pointed
to the Keno screen on the wall, newly blank.
Now, José spends his days building mah-jongg castles.

Madarika

*—Since the 20s, the International Hotel, on the edge of San Francisco's
Chinatown, had housed the* manongs—*the pioneer Filipino
immigrants to America. In 1977, young Filipino Americans fought
the eviction of these "old-timers" and the demolition of the "I-Hotel"
by linking arms against the wrecking ball—for many of them, the
event was an emblem of their awakening into Filipino-American
history and culture.*

—Madarika, *in Tagalog, means "homeless wanderer."*

You ask me my name? They got lotsa names
for me—Frankie, Manong Chito, Old-Timer—
you walk into a Chinese restaurant with me,
you see they call me "Amigo." Lotsa names.
But I'm just a Pinoy, you know? *Pinoy,*
that's a password. You see a stranger across
the street, his hair shiny with Brilliantine,
just like a rooster's dark-blue feathers after
the owner spits down the neck and head at a cockfight.
So you yell out, "Hey, Pinoy?" If the answer
come back, *"Hoy, Kababayan,"* then you know that stranger's
a friend: he'll stand at your back in a knife fight.

Anyway, my name is Francisco X. Velarde.
X for Xavier. So you see I got a powerful
patron saint. I was born in Ilocos Norte
in 1906. I still remember the sunrise
back home. I was the youngest of seven boys
and it was my job to take our *kalabaw*
to the field in the morning. I remember lying
on his broad back, gray like an elephant. The sun
climbing between his horns as he walked, first
the pink spreading across the sky like flowers.

Only another place I see something
like that was Alaska where I ended up
at a cannery in '24. It never got dark,
you know, but when the sun would sink below
the horizon, the sky would light up in purple
and pink just before sunrise. All day we slave
on the line. My job is cutting off fish heads.
One time, my *kumpadre* Paulino cuts his finger
right off but we never find it. You young Pinoys,
you never know how hard we worked at that cannery,
and it was dangerous, too. But every night
we were our own boss, and we played baseball—
fast-pitch, slow-pitch—in the midnight sun.

I worked lotsa jobs. Barber, farm
worker, dishwasher, houseboy, janitor: you name it,
I done it. Every place I been—in Alaska,
in Seattle, in Stockton cutting asparagus—
they got these dance halls. A dime for a dance.
These days, a dime don't seem like much to you,
but you know it was a lot in the 30s.
Very dear. *Mahal.* But we didn't mind.
Blondies. *Susmariosep!* We were *crazy*
for those blondies. *Ay, naku!* "No money,
no honey," they used to say. After the war,
one time, I was going out with a blondie. She had
a white fur coat down to her feet: *maganda.*
Turned out she was some kinda Russian spy,
no kidding. The FBI haul me away
and this *puti*—blond hair, blue eyes—he comes
into the room and says, *"Kumusta kayo?"*
Just like he's from Manila, and his accent's better
than mine! That time, I was working the Presidio,
folding whites in the Army hospital.
They let me go 'cause I got no top
secret to give away, you see? Believe it
or not—FBI agent talking Tagalog!

Well, I been here at the International since
long time before that blondie. I have this room
over twenty years. This same bed,
squeak squeak every night till I think
the mice are talking back. That same desk
where I used to sit and write letters back home
but I got no one there now. Same old view—
Kearny Street still the same, twenty,
thirty years. This room's all the home
I got. They kick us out, I have just one
regret: all the lotsa names I got,
no one ever called me *Lolo*. Those years
playing with blondies, I never had no kids.
And so now I can't have no grandson.
All I got is you—you college boys
ask these questions like you're doing homework.
Look around you. This is all there is.
Remember everything about this room: the smell
of old linoleum, the faded curtains,
the bugs. And when your grandkids ask about
the O.T.'s, *the* original manongs,
you tell them how we talked today. Tell them
Francisco Velarde was here. Lolo Panchito was here.

Jessica Hagedorn

Paloma Hagedorn Woo

Born and raised in the Philippines, **Jessica Hagedorn** is well known as a performance artist, poet, and playwright. Her multimedia theater pieces have been presented at New York's Public Theater, the Kitchen, Dance Theater Workshop, and St. Mark's Theater, and include *Holy Food, Teenytown,* and *Mango Tango.* She is the author of two collections of poems, prose, and short fiction, *Dangerous Music* (Momo's Press, 1975) and *Pet Food and Tropical Apparitions* (Momo's Press, 1981). Her first novel, *Dogeaters,* appeared in 1990 and was nominated for the National Book Award. For many years the leader and lyricist for the Gangster Choir band, she is presently a commentator for *Crossroads,* a syndicated weekly newsmagazine on public radio.

Smokey's Getting Old

(for Smokey Robinson)

hey Nellie,
how long you been here? did you
come with yr daddy in 1959
on a second-class boat   crying all the while
cuz you   didn't want to leave the barrio
the girls back there
who wore their hair loose
lots of orange lipstick & movies on Sundays
Quiapo market in the mornings
yr grandma chewing red tobacco
roast pig
(yeah . . . and it tastes good)

hey Nellie,
did you have to live in Stockton
with yr daddy
and talk to old farmers
who immigrated in 1941;   did yr daddy
promise you
to a fifty-eight year old bachelor
who stank of cigars
and did you run away
to San Francisco
go to Poly High
rat yr hair
hang around Woolworth's
Chinatown at three in the morning
go to the Cow Palace & catch
Smokey Robinson
cry at his gold jacket

dance
every Friday night at the Mission
go steady with Ruben
(yr daddy can't stand it
cuz he's a spik)

and the sailors
you dreamed of in Manila
with yellow hair
did they take you to the beach
to ride the ferris wheel?
Life's Never Been So Fine!

you & Carmen harmonize
"Be My Baby" by the Ronettes
and 1965 you get laid at a party
(Carmen's house)   and Ruben marries you
and you give up harmonizin'

Nellie,
you sleep without dreams
and remember the barrios
and how it's all the same

Manila,
the Mission,
Chinatown,
East L.A., Harlem, Fillmore Street,
and you're getting kinda fat
and Smokey Robinson's getting old

but yr son
has learned to jive
to the Jackson Five

"i don't want to /
but i need you / seems like /
i'm always / thinkin' of you /
though / you do me wrong now /
my love is strong / now /
you really
got a hold on me . . ."

Yolanda Meets the Wild Boys

After the paradiso and the milky way and the kosmos, seeming
as if we had all been sent to gig at some celestial city—
which, despite what some folks think, AMSTERDAM IZ NOT—we
strolled along some canal in the late night in search of that
nebulous JAZZ which might be happening in a garage
masquerading as a nightclub. I turned to lorenzo and said
(—or was it lewis? we were all walking together stoned and
speeding and exhausted)
                          "Shit—this is almost as bad as the
jazz life . . ."
                     what david murray refers to as the jazz life
y'know . . . and I **should** know, all of us here
like grinning creatures of the underworld,
poeticizing to young zombies asleep in the deep hashish maze
of netherlands bliss, borrowing from katmandu and goa,
in love with japanese hair, the waterfalls of africa
and what would my mother say if she knew? That i
shoulda had a job, vuitton luggage, a bathtub
in the george cinq hotel.
      Not this yolanda, screeching back to the wild boys
of romance, wild boys lurking in the shadows of the grimy
paradiso balcony, wild boys chanting "BULLSHIT BULLSHIT"
to all the weary poets, while yolanda yells back
                          "fuckyoutoo jack!"
tensely awaiting a confrontation that does not come.
      THE YOUNG PUNKS OF AMSTERDAM play follow-the-leader,
coming alive only when their band appears. They grab each other's
crotches, and it's an all-male show, the women highly made-up and
strangely passive. I'm feeling too old for this and don't believe much of
what i see: wearing black, young blond boys writhe around the stage floor
deliriously anti-rhythmic at the feet of their rock n'roll idol, who leaps
about and throws his hips in their faces.

"HEY THERE MUTHAFUCKAS
I'LL SHOW YOU SOME REAL ROCK N'ROLL!"
yolanda sings in english.

  The boys don't seem to care or understand. They want their
band! She pulls out
her folsom st. whip and whirls the silver microphone above
her head, like a space-age cowgirl in a rodent rodeo.
"SAY BOYS, CAN YA ONLY GET IT UP
  FOR EACH OTHER?" yolanda teases, rolling her eyes
and cracking her black whip. "HERE'S SOME REAL BLACK
    FOR YA—some san francisco
boys' town action!   The crowd is transfixed
as yolanda slashes the whip across their idol's back,
ripping off his t-shirt and drawing blood.
   "YOLANDA WANTS TO KNOW—can you
  handle it, or are we merely playing?" she grins.

  They grab each other's crotches
   and it's an all-male show,   the women
    highly made-up
     and strangely passive.

(i ask harold norse
  about marlon brando
   as we breakfast on eggs and coffee and jam that's too sweet.
   "He'd fuck anything that moves," harold replies,
    with a certain authority.   I wonder
about myself, and jeanne moreau . . . we could elope together
in the south of france and make movies . . . does patti smith spit
   every time she performs? . . . ntozake and her appetites—how
   we compare notes . . . would we really have
       any children?)

Yolanda throws back her head and laughs, strutting defiantly
across the amsterdam stage. The stage
is littered with paper cups, hurled by the wild boys from the
balcony. She picks one up and throws it back
at a bewildered audience, the boys still writhing and delirious.

"WHERE'S THE GLASS?" yolanda wants to know,
"THE BROKEN SHARDS OF GLASS? WHERE ARE
THE HALF-FINISHED BOTTLES OF BEER? DON'T THEY
ALLOW THEM HERE?"

>She shows them her high-heeled boots
>>and flicks her tongue like a desert lizard.

"LORD . . . CAN YOU
>GET IT UP, JUST SO
>>YOLANDA CAN SEE?"   She can't seem to stop laughing,
>>>shaking her long fingers
>>>like lacey fans:

>europe / europe / what
>a creature / all dis history /
>and no future . . .

The crowd becomes enraged,
pushing towards the stage. The young blond boys
climb up, running towards yolanda . . . she's standing still,
a half smile on her glistening ruby-red lips.
Yolanda sways in snakelike motion, holding the angry boys
at bay by some sort of musical hypnosis . . . her small, clear
voice singing:

>europe / europe / what
>a creature / all dis history /
>and no future . . .

The young boys remove their leather jackets and black t-shirts.
The band stops playing. IT'S YOLANDA'S SHOW, FINALLY—and she
motions for them to unzip their tight black pants.
>(Some did it, mockingly. Some did it, cursing all
>>the while. Some did it, aggressively.
>>>Some did it, with a certain surprising shyness.
>>>>But they all did it.)
Yolanda turns to the young girls in the audience, who seem
to be watching all this with a deep and mournful curiosity.
"NOW LADIES," yolanda says,
very slowly and deliberately, "IS IT SEX,

OR IS IT DEATH—or could there
be anything in between?"
     She repeats this question several times, her voice
getting louder and louder. "**IS IT SEX, OR IS IT DEATH**—
or could there be anything
in between???"
     "**Music!**" a young girl shouted.
     "**Nothing!**" another one cried.
     "**Metal!**" the women roared, mascara streaking
their pallid faces and mingling with a sudden flow of tears.
Even yolanda's eyes are wet, but she keeps grinning
as she looks at the waiting boys
some with hard-ons
some with semi hard-ons,
others without . . . their dicks
flaccid and pink,
like sleeping baby mice.
     Yolanda orders the flaccid ones to drop to their knees and work on the
semi hard-ons with their mouths. The boys who are already erect begin
touching each other, enamored with each other's obvious virility.
     Most didn't seem sure of their position. TO BEND OVER and be loved,
or to DO THE LOVING.
     Some tried to touch and grab yolanda, who easily jumped out of their
reach, gracefully avoiding the wild-eyed boys, dazzling the entire room
with her intricate r & b choreography
     "**TELL THE TRUTH TO YOURSELVES,**" yolanda says
to no one in particular. "**TELL THE TRUTH TO YOURSELVES,**
     and remember what your women have told you . . ."
With this, all
the women rose up in magnificent and beautiful fury,
screaming:
     "**MUSIC!**" "**NOTHING!**" "**METAL!**"
     Yolanda disappeared into the night and caught the first available pan-
am flight back to new york.
     I ran into her strolling down eighth street. Walking past me, she
smiled
and murmured in a sweet hoarse voice:

     "**BLACK / BLACK . . . A JOB WELL DONE.**"

Sharon Hashimoto

Sharon Hashimoto was born in Seattle in 1953. She holds Bachelor of Arts degrees from the University of Washington in modern European history and editorial journalism, as well as a Master of Fine Arts in creative writing. Currently, she is a Literature and Writing Instructor at Highline Community College. Her work has appeared in publications such as *Poetry, The American Scholar, Ironwood,* and *Carolina Quarterly,* among others. In 1989, she was a recipient of a Creative Writing Fellowship from the National Endowment for the Arts. She has completed a manuscript of poems entitled *The Crane Wife.*

The Mirror of Matsuyama

Daughter, this I give you before I die.
When you are lonely, take out this mirror.
I will be with you always.

From a Japanese folktale

Mother, what trick of light
brings you back—your face rising to the surface?
Is it my need that imprisons you behind
the cold glass? When you lay still,
the flowered quilt no longer warm with your body,
I didn't believe your promise.

                         Days passed,
and even the pauses between my breath
would remind me that you are not here.
But remembering your words, I held
your mirror before me.

                  Amazed,
you looked back, your fingers stretched
to meet mine. Between us, I could feel
only the glass. The brown centers of your eyes
returned my stare.

                    Mother, how do you see me?
Enclosed within your reflection, you can't answer
what I ask—how your teacup knows
the shape of my hands, the smooth rim
the bow of my lips. With every stroke
of my brush, why do I imagine the length
of your hair?

                  Each time we meet, we press
closer together, as if you could make me whole.

Standing in the Doorway,
I Watch the Young Child Sleep

Twenty months out of the womb,
your daughter lies still on the flat plane
of the twin bed, the sheet pulled taut
over her body like a second skin.
With her eyes closed to the dark,
does she remember the curve of your arms,
the slow pace and rhythm of your walk?
Or does she dream
of the swell and curl of the ocean,
drifting with the push of the moon,
the pull of the sun? That night,
you whimpered and clutched
at your pillow. Opening your eyes
to the dead quiet of the house,
you shrank away from the window
where a full moon hung pierced
on an apple tree's thin branches.
Your daughter rubs her cheek with her hand
and I can see our mother folding you
close into the creases of elbow and lap,
resting your head between the hills
of her breasts. Here, in this one shade
of night stretched over the room,
I can almost feel our mother's warm breath
as she leaned forward,
hiding your face
behind a fall of black hair.

Eleven A.M. on My Day Off, My Sister Phones Desperate for a Babysitter

Sitting in sunlight, the child
I sometimes pretend is my own
fingers the green weave of the rug
while the small shadow of her head falls over
a part of my lap and bent knee. At three,
she could be that younger part of myself, just beginning
to remember how the dusty warmth feels on her back.
"Are you hungry?" I ask. Together we open
the door of the refrigerator. One apple sits
in the vegetable bin but she gives it to me,
repeating her true mother's words "to share."
Turning the round fruit under the faucet,
the afternoon bright in my face, I look down
at a smile in the half moons of her eyes
and for a moment, I'm seven, looking up
at my childless aunt in Hawaii,
her hands and the long knife peeling
the mango I picked off the tree, rubbing my arms
from the stretch on the back porch
to an overhead branch. Plump
with the island's humidity, it tasted tart
like the heavy clatter of rain on a June Sunday.
"Careful," my niece warns as I slice the apple sideways
to show her the star in the middle.
She eats the core but saves the seeds
to plant in the soft earth of my yard.

Garrett Hongo

Gary Tepfer

Garrett Hongo is the editor of this volume and author of *Yellow Light* (1982) and *The River of Heaven* (1988). In the mid-seventies, he was founder and director of the Asian Exclusion Act, a Seattle theater company. He now lives in Eugene, Oregon, with his wife, Cynthia Thiessen, a violinist, and their two children, Alexander and Hudson.

Yellow Light

One arm hooked around the frayed strap
of a tar-black patent-leather purse,
the other cradling something for dinner:
fresh bunches of spinach from a J-Town *yaoya,*
sides of split Spanish mackerel from Alviso's,
maybe a loaf of Langendorf; she steps
off the hissing bus at Olympic and Fig,
begins the three-block climb up the hill,
passing gangs of schoolboys playing war,
Japs against Japs, Chicanas chalking sidewalks
with the holy double-yoked crosses of hopscotch,
and the Korean grocer's wife out for a stroll
around this neighborhood of Hawaiian apartments
just starting to steam with cooking
and the anger of young couples coming home
from work, yelling at kids, flicking on
TV sets for the Wednesday Night Fights.

If it were May, hydrangeas and jacaranda
flowers in the streetside trees would be
blooming through the smog of late spring.
Wisteria in Masuda's front yard would be
shaking out the long tresses of its purple hair.
Maybe mosquitoes, moths, a few orange butterflies
settling on the lattice of monkey flowers
tangled in chain-link fences by the trash.

But this is October, and Los Angeles
seethes like a billboard under twilight.
From used-car lots and the movie houses uptown,
long silver sticks of light probe the sky.
From the Miracle Mile, whole freeways away,
a brilliant fluorescence breaks out
and makes war with the dim squares
of yellow kitchen light winking on
in all the side streets of the Barrio.

She climbs up the two flights of flagstone
stairs to 201-B, the spikes of her high heels
clicking like kitchen knives on a cutting board,
props the groceries against the door,
fishes through memo pads, a compact,
empty packs of chewing gum, and finds her keys.

The moon then, cruising from behind
a screen of eucalyptus across the street,
covers everything, everything in sight,
in a heavy light like yellow onions.

Winnings

It's Gardena, late Saturday afternoon
on Vermont Avenue, near closing time
at the thrift store, and my father's
left me to rummage through trash bins
stuffed with used paperbacks, 25¢ a pound,
while he chases down some bets
at the card clubs across the street.

The register rings up its sales—$2.95,
$11.24, $26.48 for the reclaimed Frigidaire—
and a girl, maybe six or so, barefoot,
in a plaid dress, her hair braided
in tight cornrows, tugs at the strap
of her mother's purse, begging a few
nickels for the gumball machine.

She skips through the check-stand,
runs toward the electric exit, passing
a fleet of shopping carts, bundles
of used-up magazines *(Ebony* and *Jet)*
stacked in pyramids in the far aisle,
reaches the bright globe of the vendor,
fumbles for her coins, and works the knob.

My father comes in from the Rainbow
across the street, ten hands of Jacks
or Better, five draw, a winner
with a few dollars to peel away
from grocery money and money to fix
the washer, a dollar for me to buy
four pounds of Pocket Wisdoms, Bantams,
a Dell that says *Walt Whitman, Poet
of the Open Road,* and hands it to me,

saying "We won, *Boy-san*! We won!"
as the final blast of sunset kicks through
plate glass and stained air, firing through
the thicket of neon across the street,
consuming the store, the girl, the dollar bill,

even the Rainbow and the falling night
in a brief symphony of candied light.

The Unreal Dwelling: My Years in Volcano

What I did, I won't excuse, except
to say it was a way to change,
the way new flows add to the land,
making things new, clearing the garden.
I left two sons, a wife behind—
and does it matter? The sons grew,
became their own kinds of men,
lost in the swirl of robes, cries
behind a screen of mist and fire
I drew between us, gambles I lost
and walked away from like any bad job.
I drove a cab and didn't care,
let the wife run off too, her combs
loose in some shopkeeper's bed.
When hope blazed up in my heart for the fresh start,
I took my daughters with me to keep house,
order my living as I was taught and came to expect.
They swept up, cooked, arranged flowers,
practiced tea and *buyō,* the classical dance.
I knew how because I could read and ordered books,
let all movements be disciplined and objects arranged
by an idea of order, the precise sequence of images
which conjure up the abstract I might call
yūgen, or Mystery, *chikara* . . . Power.
The principles were in the swordsmanship
I practiced, in the package of loans
and small thefts I'd managed since coming here.
I could count, keep books, speak English
as well as any white, and I had false papers
recommending me, celebrating the fiction
of my long tenure with Hata Shōten of Honolulu.
And my luck was they bothered to check
only those I'd bribed or made love to.

Charm was my collateral, a willingness to move
and live on the frontier my strongest selling point.
So they staked me, a small-time hustler
good with cars, odds, and women,
and I tossed some boards together,
dug ponds and a cesspool,
figured water needed tanks, pipes,
and guttering on the eaves
to catch the light-falling rain,
and I had it—a store and house out-back
carved out of rainforests and lava land
beside this mountain road seven leagues from Hilo.
I never worried they'd come this far—
the banks, courts, and police—
mists and sulphur clouds from the crater
drenching the land, washing clean my tracks,
bleaching my spotted skin the pallor of long-time residents.
I regularized my life and raised my girls,
put in gas pumps out front, stocked varieties of goods
and took in local fruit, flowers on consignment.
And I had liquor—plum wine and *saké*
from Japan, whiskey from Tennessee—
which meant I kept a pistol as well.
My girls learned to shoot, and would have
only no one bothered to test us.
It was known I'd shot cats and wild pigs
from across the road rummaging through garbage.
I never thought of my boys,
or of women too much until my oldest bloomed,
suddenly, vanda-like, from spike
to scented flower almost overnight.
Young men in model A's came up from town.
One even bused, and a Marine from Georgia
stole a Jeep to try taking her
to the coast, or, more simply,
down a mountain road for the night.
The Shore Patrol found him.
And I got married again, to a country girl

from Kona who answered my ad.
I approved of her because,
though she was rough-spoken and squat-legged,
and, I discovered, her hair
slightly red in the groin,
she could carry 50-lb. sacks of California Rose
without strain or grunting.
As postmaster and Territorial official,
I married us myself, sent announcements
and champagne in medicine vials
to the villagers and my "guarantors" in town.
The toasts tasted of vitamin B and cough syrup.
My oldest moved away, herself married
to a dapper Okinawan who sold Oldsmobiles
and had the leisure to play golf on weekends.
I heard from my boy then, my oldest son,
back from the war and writing to us,
curious, formal, and not a little proud
he'd done his part. What impressed me
was his script—florid but under control,
penmanship like pipers at the tideline
lifting and settling on the sand-colored paper.
He wrote first from Europe, then New York,
finally from Honolulu. He'd fought,
mustered out near the Madison Square Garden
in time to see LaMotta smash the pretty one,
and then came home to a girl he'd met in night school.
He said he won out over a cop because he danced better,
knew from the service how to show up in a tie,
bring flowers and silk in nice wrappings.
I flew the Island Clipper to the wedding,
the first time I'd seen the boy in twenty years,
gave him a hundred cash and a wink
since the girl was pretty,
told him to buy, not rent his suits,
and came home the next day, hung over,
a raw ache in my throat.
I sobered up, but the ache

stayed and doctors tell me
it's this sickness they can't get rid of,
pain all through my blood and nerve cells.
I cough too much, can't smoke or drink
or tend to things. Mornings, I roll
myself off the damp bed, wrap
a blanket on, slip into the wooden clogs,
and take a walk around my pond and gardens.
On this half-acre, calla lilies in bloom,
cream-white cups swollen with milk,
heavy on their stems and rocking in the slight wind,
cranes coming to rest on the wet, coppery soil.
The lotuses ride, tiny flamingoes, sapphired
pavilions buoyed on their green keels on the pond.
My fish follow me, snorting to be fed,
gold flashes and streaks of color
like blood satin and brocade in the algaed waters.
And when the sky empties of its many lights,
I see the quarter moon, horned junk,
sailing over Ka'ū and the crater rim.
This is the River of Heaven. . . .
Before I cross, I know I must bow down,
call to my oldest son, say what I must
to bring him, and all the past, back to me.

The Pier

In winter, those first mornings after my father died,
I'd get out of the apartment and take walks
along the boardwalk while the wind scuffed
over low dunes on the deserted beach
and skipped trash through alleyways
I walked through on my way to the pier.
Coastal fog would sometimes shroud everything—
the few motels, small cottages miscellaneous in design,
the Bauhaus beachshack absurd with its concrete stilts
and assortment of cutout windows and color panels
like a make-up tray styled by Mondrian—
as if some gray ghost of a manta or skate
had, overnight, chosen this beachtown as its bottom
and settled, wraithlike, over all its weather and dilapidation.
Or, it would have stormed for days,
or a storm would be on its way, the pioneer
or remnant clouds like huge purple swans
gliding across the channel from Catalina
over the choppy aquamarine to the inland plains,
trailing their small skirts of rain and glory
past buzzing power lines flexing in the strong, on-shore wind.
Up on the pier, by the glassed-in lifeguard station,
I'd see couples in ski parkas and peacoats clenched against
                                        each other
while a few gulls hovered overhead, hoarding the wind,
screeching their mild complaints. I'd see fishermen
waddle by burdened with plastic buckets filled with bait
or their poor catch of leopard sharks and Spanish mackerel,
the black, swordlike bracts and blossoms of their tails
drooping like loose bunches of glutinous flowers over the rims.
I had no heart, I felt nothing, could think
only that I didn't believe he'd died
so close to making it through—retirement
just around the two-year corner like a beacon

cutting through the gray present, the best moments
of our friendship, silent as the burst of yellow light
like a brushfire catching in all the windows
up the far, west-facing shore at sunset,
still ahead for us, loomings riding under cloud-cover,
a rosy blaze reaching out to small crafts at sea.
I'd see Vietnamese in small, family groups,
or they were Cambodians—Asians as foreign to me
as my grandfathers might have been
to the Yank seaman who stared, stopped
in his climb up the worn rigging of his tall ship,
as they tramped in wooden clogs off the *City of Tokio*
and down the "China Bridge," a long, wooden plank,
over marshy land to the Immigration Station
at Honolulu Bay. They'd be mothering handlines over the railing,
jigging a "Christmas tree" of small, feathered hooks
to catch the baitfish they'd need for the mackerel,
bonito, and flounder cruising the musseled pilings
in the green waters frothing under the pier.
For splendor, for his cheap fun, my father
would go to the track, lose himself in the crowd
milling around the paddock, weighing the odds
against the look of the horse, handicapping,
exchanging tips, rushing the window just before post-time
and rising to his feet for the stretch run,
beating cadence and whipping a gabardine pants leg
in rhythm and chant to the jockey's ride.
I think splendor must be something of what we all want
somehow, respite from privation and a world
of diminishment, a small drama so strange
it exiles the common yet thrills us with our own stories:
the mother, having lost her child, who sees,
through reeds on the riverbank, a glimpse
of the boy her child might have become,
and then herself is swept away in the river's next flooding;
the drunk who constructs, in a series of baroque fantasies,
the fabulous mansion with its Moroccan pool
surrounded by wrought-iron gates and fences, magnificently Byzantine,
while he lives out his life on the edge of a junkyard

by the drive-in, in the hulk of an abandoned automobile;
or, the poor painter who steps out from behind a woodpile
after chapel one day to denounce his younger brother,
himself a master of religious painting,
accusing him of pride and falsity, destroying his brother's faith,
gaining a small advantage and the impermanent rise of his own
                                        reputation;
or, my favorite, the young voluptuary, frigid in her marriage bed,
who flees on a winter's night through barren woods,
escaping her peasant husband, the village, and this life,
stripping nude at riverside and plunging in,
beginning an alabaster, fetal crawl through the roiling
                                        green waters
collapsing in mock pleasure around her as she drowns,
engulfed by the image of a rising moon
breaking up and coming together again
on the slick, mutable surface of the water.
My father believed in what he could imagine for himself—
a set of numbers written like calligraphy on a handicap sheet
that translated into his occasional but regular movements
through a world made beautiful by his own need
for that beauty and its sequence of splendid events,
desire that metamorphosed into scenario after scenario
and their ritual demarcations—swans gliding
on the infield pond while a trumpet blared its call—
while that other world went on with its load of pain,
its twelvescore of humiliations and ridicule.
These immigrants, on workdays, line a certain street
up in Costa Mesa on the bluff, stationing themselves
like whores at a bus stop, while cars cruise by,
suburban wagons and Euro-sedans, housewives at the wheel,
picking and choosing their day-domestics
from the lineup of illegals and boat people
begging for work, grinning at each electric window
as cars drive up, stop, and a matron leans out,
negotiates a price, opening a back door
and waving them in, or else demurs, passing all of them by,
gliding along in her polished, nearly perfect world.

The Legend

In Chicago, it is snowing softly
and a man has just done his wash for the week.
He steps into the twilight of early evening,
carrying a wrinkled shopping bag
full of neatly folded clothes,
and, for a moment, enjoys
the feel of warm laundry and crinkled paper,
flannellike against his gloveless hands.
There's a Rembrandt glow on his face,
a triangle of orange in the hollow of his cheek
as a last flash of sunset
blazes the storefronts and lit windows of the street.

He is Asian, Thai or Vietnamese,
and very skinny, dressed as one of the poor
in rumpled suit pants and a plaid mackinaw,
dingy and too large.
He negotiates the slick of ice
on the sidewalk by his car,
opens the Fairlane's back door,
leans to place the laundry in,
and turns, for an instant,
toward the flurry of footsteps
and cries of pedestrians
as a boy—that's all he was—
backs from the corner package store
shooting a pistol, firing it,
once, at the dumbfounded man
who falls forward,
grabbing at his chest.

A few sounds escape from his mouth,
a babbling no one understands
as people surround him
bewildered at his speech.
The noises he makes are nothing to them.
The boy has gone, lost
in the light array of foot traffic
dappling the snow with fresh prints.

Tonight, I read about Descartes'
grand courage to doubt everything
except his own miraculous existence
and I feel so distinct
from the wounded man lying on the concrete
I am ashamed.

Let the night sky cover him as he dies.
Let the weaver girl cross the bridge of heaven
and take up his cold hands.

In Memory of Jay Kashiwamura

Lawson Fusao Inada

Lawson Fusao Inada is the author of *Before the War* (William Morrow, 1971). He is an editor of two Asian American anthologies, *Aiiieeeee!* (Doubleday, 1976) and *The Big Aiiieeeee!* (New American Library, 1991). With Garrett Hongo and Alan Chong Lau, he wrote *The Buddha Bandits Down Highway 99* (Buddahead Press, 1978). He has received two fellowships from the National Endowment for the Arts, has served on the Literature Panel for the Endowment, and is currently serving on the Commission on Racism and Bias in Education for the National Council of Teachers of English. He is a Professor of English at Southern Oregon State College. He and his wife, Janet, have two sons, Miles and Lowell.

The Great Bassist

For Charles Mingus

I am the Great Bassist:
music, life, are one.
And it is fine.

It wasn't always that way . . .

When I was young,
music plugged my veins
and wouldn't run.

I bought a bass
and practiced.

Nothing would come:

wire
lanced the flesh only—
that ache inside,
unletting—

lacerations
of a master's whip
cutting
down through the calluses,
society in the cracks
like salt and pepper . . .

Then bass was woman;
I, her master.

She was black, Africa's
shape
misshapened. We made
love like hate.
We bled
all over each other.
I plucked
her guts until we almost died . . .

One night, I saw a light
shouldering the horizon—

a light we made.

It accompanied us.

And when the blues
came down like rain,
we played
away the rain,
and love fell
into place like syllogisms . . .

The best of nights, we made
sea-rhythm, pulse
of wave strength
lapping sand.

Moon and earth, each
of the other, we strummed
telephone wires in a cold field—

music like blood
rushing, blood of all peoples,

humming, rushing . . .

I am in Levi's now—
that doesn't matter.

And when I walk the streets
wind
flattens my beard
and I look tired, tattered.

That doesn't matter.

But I need your love.
We need
each other.

So when I come down your street
with my Great Bass—

toss us your love—

we'll play you
love petals.

Love us back.

If you don't we'll kill you.

All of you.

We will.

Filling the Gap

When Bird died, I didn't mind:
I had things to do—

polish some shoes, practice
a high school cha-cha-cha.

I didn't even know
Clifford was dead:

I must have been
lobbing an oblong ball
beside the gymnasium.

I saw the Lady
right before she died—

dried, brittle
as last year's gardenia.

I let her scratch an autograph.

But not Pres.

Too bugged to boo, I left
as Basie's brass
booted him off the stand
in a sick reunion—

tottering, saxophone
dragging him like a stage-hook.

When I read Dr. Williams'
poem, "Stormy,"
I wrote a letter of love and praise

and didn't mail it.

After he died, it burned my desk
like a delinquent prescription . . .

I don't like to mourn the dead:
what didn't, never will.

And I sometimes feel foolish
staying up late,
trying to squeeze some life
out of books and records,
filling the gaps
between words and notes.

That is why
I rush into our room to find you
mumbling and moaning
in your incoherent performance.

That is why
I rub and squeeze you
and love to hear your
live, alterable cry against my breast.

Maxine Hong Kingston

Jane Scherr

Maxine Hong Kingston is the author of two earlier books: *The Woman Warrior—Memoirs of a Girlhood Among Ghosts,* winner of the National Book Critics Circle Award for nonfiction, and *China Men,* winner of the National Book Award for nonfiction. She is also the author of the novel *Tripmaster Monkey—His Fake Book.* She lives in Oakland, California, and is married to Earll Kingston, an actor; they have a son, Joseph Kingston, a musician.

Restaurant

for Lilah Kan

The main cook lies sick on a banquette, and his assistant
has cut his thumb. So the quiche cook takes
their places at the eight-burner range, and you and I
get to roll out twenty-three rounds of pie
dough and break a hundred eggs, four at a crack,
and sift out shell with a China cap, pack
spinach in the steel sink, squish and squeeze
the water out, and grate a full moon of cheese.
Pam, the pastry chef, who is baking Choco-
late Globs (once called Mulattos) complains about the disco,
which Lewis, the salad man, turns up louder out of spite.
"Black so called musician." "Broads. Whites."
The porters, who speak French, from the Ivory Coast,
sweep up droppings and wash the pans without soap.
We won't be out of here until three a.m. In this basement,
I lose my size. I am a bent-over
child, Gretel or Jill, and I can
lift a pot as big as a tub with both hands.
Using a pitchfork, you stoke the broccoli and bacon.
Then I find you in the freezer, taking
a nibble of a slab of chocolate as big as a table.
We put the quiches in the oven, then we are able
to stick our heads up out of the sidewalk into the night
and wonder at the clean diners behind glass in candlelight.

Absorption of Rock

We bought from Laotian refugees a cloth
that in war a woman sewed, appliquéd
700 triangles—mountain ranges
changing colors with H'mong suns and seasons,
white and yellow teeth, black arrows,
or sails. They point in at an embroidery,
whose mystery seems the same as that posed
by face cards. Up close, the curls and x's do
not turn plainer; a green strand runs through
the yellow chains, and black between the white.
Sometimes caught from across the room, twilighted,
the lace in the center smokes, and shadows move
over the red background, which should shine.
One refugee said, "This is old woman's design."

We rented a room to a Vietnam vet,
who one Saturday night ran back to it—
thrashed through bamboo along the neighborhood
stream, then out on to sidewalk, lost the police,
though he imprinted the cement with blood
from his cut foot. He came out of the bathroom
an unidentifiable man. His strange
jagged wound yet unstaunched, he had shaved.
Yellow beard was mixed with blood and what
looked like bits of skin in the tub and toilet.
On the way to the hospital, he said, "Today
the M.C. raised his finger part way.
They're just about ready to gong my act."

We search out facts to defend a Vietnamese,
who has allegedly shot to death a Lao
in Stockton, outside a bar. It was in fear,
we hear him say, of a cantaloupe or rock

that the Lao man had caused to appear
inside him. One anthropologist testifies
that Vietnamese driving in the highlands
rolled up the windows against the H'mong air.
The H'mong in Fairfield were not indicted for
their try at family suicide; there was a question
of a Lao curse or want of a telephone.
Three translators have run away—this fourth
does not say enough words.

Alan Chong Lau

Alvin Eng

Alan Chong Lau was born in 1948 and obtained his B.A. in art from the University of California, Santa Cruz, in 1976. With Lawson Fusao Inada and Garrett Hongo, he wrote *The Buddha Bandits Down Highway 99* (Buddhahead Press, 1978). His book, *Songs for Jadina* (Greenfield Review Press, 1980), won an American Book Award from the Before Columbus Foundation. In 1983, he received a Japan-U.S. Creative Artists Fellowship under the joint sponsorship of the Japan-U.S. Friendship Commission, National Endowment for the Arts, and the Agency for Cultural Affairs of the Japanese Government.

three sketches from
The American Restaurant—
el dorado street, stockton, 1944

for my mother who grew up there

1 the evidence of men's shoes and speech

a curious drawing in shades of brown, gray, red, and blue /
moves across the wall below the counter / in order of reflex
and stretch, stub and smear, skid, kick, and final spurt of
anger / i know because i clean out the spittoons / line them up
neatly beside the graceless stems of each red swivel top in the
morning / brass containers that catch more than you see / the
argument of speech in periods and exclamation points / the
hacks of a cough that consumes / the ashes of stunted desire
leaping off a cigarette in slow motion / and bending over to
empty each spittoon / i notice the haphazard waltz of men's
shoes / the scuff marks of an oxford reminds me of faint scars
ready to disappear / the points of wingtips seem to fly in easy
arcs / the cut of glass on a bruised bare foot says red in a
child's scrawl / and finally the lines of workboots / sturdy in
their imprint / leaves the smudge of soil they carry in fields
before sunrise / staring at the wall where this afternoon's feet
leave a trail of their movement / i pick up a crayon and draw
my own path into the light melting out the screen door / as
flies bask in what remains /

2 better than nothing at all

the odor of grease and human salt wears the walls of the
restaurant / the chatter of conversation mingles with the
thrash of rice in a wok / the sizzle of spam reacting to a grill /
and the buzz of flies around the fans / it is in the evening just
after dusk when the streets carry unreal shades of day's burial
that men fill the restaurant / swollen with sound and a cush-

ion of bodies swaying to similar rhythms / even the room begins to breathe / takes on the form of its occupants / wheezing like a giant accordion whose notes are as numerous as voices / this is especially so on payday / when the hunger for things temporary / is better than nothing at all /

3 the octopus

it is over before i know what i see / a motion so quick that there is only a grin of steel / that catches a blink of the eye / only a whispered groan as a man straddles a stool / his hands and feet dangle down like four legs of a lost octopus / as the seat turns around and around squeaking a melody of its own / the starched blue shirt begins to flower in a pond of red / like a sponge drinks up a stain / i stand mesmerized / unable to take my eyes off the way color blossoms in his chest / the way it floods his body / threatens to dye the whole fabric / the first and last murder i will ever see / even the wet hair of the mop is never the same again / as it drags its feet across the floor / in a breath of steam /

my ship does not need a helmsman

"a ship depends upon
its helmsman for direction
the great ship china
is guided by mao tse tung"
—as seen on the entrance to one of
    the floors of the people's republic
    of china department store—
    kowloon, hong kong

1

here i lie in chinatown
coughing into my mattress
soaked with the odours
of salted fish
dark years old

home is not
never was
this graygreased
smokefilled room

the walls
smell the same
as the rotting wood crates
from china
that lie piled
with my memories
buried under old papers
of sun yat sen
scented with mothballs

i go outside
and spit
throwing up specks of blood
half cooked soystained rice
for the insistent pigeons

i am a sick dog
and though my tongue
lies continually out
my tail remains standing

2

the young ones
born here
or f.o.b. (fresh off the boat)
snot dripping from the nose
asses strutting
under the streetlamps
simply regard me
as old man
which means docile dog

i know it
don't think i don't know it
but my heart
is not in the fight
of children

it lies in the bones
and ashes of my wife
who died waiting
in the home of my province
feeding the ducks
staining her apron

the young barbarians
urge me to protest
in a western style
this gray life

they thrust red books in my face
but i see nothing
except the pigeons
leaving droppings
on my bench

they do not realize
i would rather
withdraw from what
i have never belonged to
than to embrace it

3

here i lie in chinatown
may the rain soak
my ashes

may the muddy rivers
carry them home
to my province

a ship does not need
a helmsman
only a woman
who strokes my brow
and laughs
at the moon
when it is full

Li-Young Lee

Li-Young Lee was born in 1957 in Jakarta, Indonesia, of Chinese descent and came to the United States at the age of six. He studied at the University of Pittsburgh, the University of Arizona, and the State University of New York at Brockport. His honors include grants from the Illinois Arts Council, The Commonwealth of Pennsylvania, the Pennsylvania Council on the Arts, and the National Endowment for the Arts. In 1988, he was the recipient of a Writer's Award from the Mrs. Giles Whiting Foundation, and in 1989, he was awarded a fellowship by the Guggenheim Foundation. His first book, *Rose* (BOA Editions, 1986), received New York University's Delmore Schwartz Memorial Poetry Award. His second book, *The City in Which I Love You* (BOA Editions, 1990), was the 1990 Lamont Poetry Selection of the Academy of American Poets. Currently, he resides in Chicago with his wife, Donna, and their two children.

The Gift

To pull the metal splinter from my palm
my father recited a story in a low voice.
I watched his lovely face and not the blade.
Before the story ended, he'd removed
the iron sliver I thought I'd die from.

I can't remember the tale,
but hear his voice still, a well
of dark water, a prayer.
And I recall his hands,
two measures of tenderness
he laid against my face,
the flames of discipline
he raised above my head.

Had you entered that afternoon
you would have thought you saw a man
planting something in a boy's palm,
a silver tear, a tiny flame.
Had you followed that boy
you would have arrived here,
where I bend over my wife's right hand.

Look how I shave her thumbnail down
so carefully she feels no pain.
Watch as I lift the splinter out.
I was seven when my father
took my hand like this,
and I did not hold that shard
between my fingers and think,
Metal that will bury me,
christen it Little Assassin,
Ore Going Deep for My Heart.

And I did not lift up my wound and cry,
Death visited here!
I did what a child does
when he's given something to keep.
I kissed my father.

The Cleaving

He gossips like my grandmother, this man
with my face, and I could stand
amused all afternoon
in the Hon Kee Grocery,
amid hanging meats he
chops: roast pork cut
from a hog hung
by nose and shoulders,
her entire skin burnt
crisp, flesh I know
to be sweet,
her shining
face grinning
up at ducks
dangling single file,
each pierced by black
hooks through breast, bill,
and steaming from a hole
stitched shut at the ass.
I step to the counter, recite,
and he, without even slightly
varying the rhythm of his current confession or harangue,
scribbles my order on a greasy receipt,
and chops it up quick.

Such a sorrowful Chinese face,
nomad, Gobi, Northern
in its boniness
clear from the high
warlike forehead
to the sheer edge of the jaw.
He could be my brother, but finer,
and, except for his left forearm, which is engorged,

sinewy from his daily grip and
wield of a two-pound tool,
he's delicate, narrow-
waisted, his frame
so slight a lover, some
rough other
might break it down
its smooth, oily length.
In his light-handed calligraphy
on receipts and in his
moodiness, he is
a Southerner from a river-province;
suited for scholarship, his face poised
above an open book, he'd mumble
his favorite passages.
He could be my grandfather;
come to America to get a Western education
in 1917, but too homesick to study,
he sits in the park all day, reading poems
and writing letters to his mother.

He lops the head off, chops
the neck of the duck
into six, slits
the body
open, groin
to breast, and drains
the scalding juices,
then quarters the carcass
with two fast hacks of the cleaver,
old blade that has worn
into the surface of the round
foot-thick chop-block
a scoop that cradles precisely the curved steel.

The head, flung from the body, opens
down the middle where the butcher
cleanly halved it between
the eyes, and I
see, foetal-crouched
inside the skull, the homunculus,
gray brain grainy
to eat.
Did this animal, after all, at the moment
its neck broke,
image the way his executioner
shrinks from his own death?
Is this how
I, too, recoil from my day?
See how this shape
hordes itself, see how
little it is.
See its grease on the blade.
Is this how I'll be found
when judgement is passed, when names
are called, when crimes are tallied?
This is also how I looked before I tore my mother open.
Is this how I presided over my century, is this how
I regarded the murders?
This is also how I prayed.
Was it me in the Other
I prayed to when I prayed?
This too was how I slept, clutching my wife.
Was it me in the other I loved
when I loved another?
The butcher sees me eye this delicacy.
With a finger, he picks it
out of the skull-cradle
and offers it to me.
I take it gingerly between my fingers
and suck it down.
I eat my man.

The noise the body makes
when the body meets
the soul over the soul's ocean and penumbra
is the old sound of up-and-down, in-and-out,
a lump of muscle chug-chugging blood
into the ear; a lover's
heart-shaped tongue;
flesh rocking flesh until flesh comes;
the butcher working
at his block and blade to marry their shapes
by violence and time;
an engine crossing,
re-crossing salt water, hauling
immigrants and the junk
of the poor. These
are the faces I love, the bodies
and scents of bodies
for which I long
in various ways, at various times,
thirteen gathered around the redwood,
happy, talkative, voracious
at day's end,
eager to eat
four kinds of meat
prepared four different ways,
numerous plates and bowls of rice and vegetables,
each made by distinct affections
and brought to table by many hands.
Brothers and sisters by blood and design,
who sit in separate bodies of varied shapes,
we constitute a many-membered
body of love.
In a world of shapes
of my desires, each one here
is a shape of one of my desires, and each
is known to me and dear by virtue
of each one's unique corruption
of those texts, the face, the body:

that jut jaw
to gnash tendon;
that wide nose to meet the blows
a face like that invites;
those long eyes closing on the seen;
those thick lips
to suck the meat of animals
or recite 300 poems of the T'ang;
these teeth to bite my monosyllables;
these cheekbones to make
those syllables sing the soul.
Puffed or sunken
according to the life,
dark or light according
to the birth, straight
or humped, whole, manqué, quasi, each pleases, verging
on utter grotesquery.
All are beautiful by variety.
The soul too
is a debasement
of a text, but, thus, it
acquires salience, although a
human salience, but
inimitable, and, hence, memorable.
God is the text.
The soul is a corruption
and a mnemonic.

A bright moment,
I hold up an old head
from the sea and admire the haughty
down-curved mouth
that seems to disdain
all the eyes are blind to,
including me, the eater.
Whole unto itself, complete
without me, yet its
shape complements the shape of my mind.

I take it as text and evidence
of the world's love for me,
and I feel urged to utterance,
urged to read the body of the world, urged
to say it
in human terms,
my reading a kind of eating, my eating
a kind of reading,
my saying a diminishment, my noise
a love-in-answer.
What is it in me would
devour the world to utter it?
What is it in me will not let
the world be, would eat
not just this fish,
but the one who killed it,
the butcher who cleaned it.
I would eat the way he
squats, the way he
reaches into the plastic tubs
and pulls out a fish, clubs it, takes it
to the sink, guts it, drops it on the weighing pan.
I would eat that thrash
and plunge of the watery body
in the water, that liquid violence
between the man's hands,
I would eat
the gutless twitching on the scales,
three pounds of dumb
nerve and pulse, I would eat it all
to utter it.
The deaths at the sinks, those bodies prepared
for eating, I would eat,
and the standing deaths
at the counters, in the aisles,
the walking deaths in the streets,
the death-far-from-home, the death-
in-a-strange-land, these Chinatown

deaths, these American deaths.
I would devour this race to sing it,
this race that according to Emerson
managed to preserve to a hair
for three or four thousand years
the ugliest features in the world.
I would eat these features, eat
the last three or four thousand years, every hair.
And I would eat Emerson, his transparent soul, his
soporific transcendence.
I would eat this head,
glazed in pepper-speckled sauce,
the cooked eyes opaque in their sockets.
I bring it to my mouth and—
the way I was taught, the way I've watched
others before me do—
with a stiff tongue lick out
the cheek-meat and the meat
over the armored jaw, my eating,
its sensual, salient nowness,
punctuating the void
from which such hunger springs and to which it proceeds.

And what
is this
I excavate
with my mouth?
What is this
plated, ribbed, hinged
architecture, this *carp head,*
but one more
articulation of a single nothing
severally manifested?
What is my eating,
rapt as it is,
but another
shape of going,
my immaculate expiration?

O, nothing is so
steadfast it won't go
the way the body goes.
The body goes.
The body's grave,
so serious
in its dying,
arduous as martyrs
in that task and as
glorious. It goes
empty always
and announces its going
by spasms and groans, farts and sweats.

What I thought were the arms
aching *cleave,* were the knees trembling *leave.*
What I thought were the muscles
insisting *resist, persist, exist,*
were the pores
hissing *mist* and *waste.*
What I thought was the body humming *reside, reside,*
was the body sighing *revise, revise.*
O, the murderous deletions, the keening
down to nothing, the cleaving.
All of the body's revisions end
in death.
All of the body's revisions end.

Bodies eating bodies, heads eating heads,
we are nothing eating nothing,
and though we feast,
are filled, overfilled,
we go famished.
We gang the doors of death.
That is, our deaths are fed
that we may continue our daily dying,
our bodies going
down, while the plates-soon-empty

are passed around, that true
direction of our true prayers,
while the butcher spells
his message, manifold,
in the mortal air.
He coaxes, cleaves, brings change
before our very eyes, and at every
moment of our being.
As we eat we're eaten.
Else what is this
violence, this salt, this
passion, this heaven?

I thought the soul an airy thing.
I did not know the soul
is cleaved so that the soul might be restored.
Live wood hewn,
its sap springs from a sticky wound.
No seed, no egg has he
whose business calls for an axe.
In the trade of my soul's shaping,
he traffics in hews and hacks.

No easy thing, violence.
One of its names? Change. Change
resides in the embrace
of the effaced and the effacer,
in the covenant of the opened and the opener;
the axe accomplishes it on the soul's axis.
What then may I do
but cleave to what cleaves me.
I kiss the blade and eat my meat.
I thank the wielder and receive,
while terror spirits
my change, sorrow also.
The terror the butcher
scripts in the unhealed
air, the sorrow of his Shang

dynasty face,
African face with slit eyes. He is
my sister, this
beautiful Bedouin, this Shulamite,
keeper of sabbaths, diviner
of holy texts, this dark
dancer, this Jew, this Asian, this one
with the Cambodian face, Vietnamese face, this Chinese
I daily face,
this immigrant,
this man with my own face.

This Room and Everything in It

Lie still now
while I prepare for my future,
certain hard days ahead,
when I'll need what I know so clearly this moment.

I am making use
of the one thing I learned
of all the things my father tried to teach me:
the art of memory.

I am letting this room
and everything in it
stand for my ideas about love
and its difficulties.

I'll let your love-cries,
those spacious notes
of a moment ago,
stand for distance.

Your scent,
that scent
of spice and a wound,
I'll let stand for mystery.

Your sunken belly
is the daily cup
of milk I drank
as a boy before morning prayer.

The sun on the face
of the wall
is God, the face
I can't see, my soul,

and so on, each thing
standing for a separate idea,
and those ideas forming the constellation
of my greater idea.
And one day, when I need
to tell myself something intelligent
about love,

I'll close my eyes
and recall this room and everything in it:
My body is estrangement.
This desire, perfection.
Your closed eyes my extinction.
Now I've forgotten my
idea. The book
on the windowsill, riffled by wind . . .
the even-numbered pages are
the past, the odd-
numbered pages, the future.
The sun is
God, your body is milk . . .

useless, useless . . .
your cries are song, my body's not me . . .
no good . . . my idea
has evaporated . . . your hair is time, your thighs are song . . .
it had something to do
with death . . . it had something
to do with love.

I Ask My Mother to Sing

She begins, and my grandmother joins her.
Mother and daughter sing like young girls.
If my father were alive, he would play
his accordion and sway like a boat.

I've never been in Peking, or the Summer Palace,
nor stood on the great Stone Boat to watch
the rain begin on Kuen Ming Lake, the picnickers
running away in the grass.

But I love to hear it sung;
how the waterlilies fill with rain until
they overturn, spilling water into water,
then rock back, and fill with more.

Both women have begun to cry.
But neither stops her song.

Russell Leong

Tu Ying-Ming

Russell Leong: "Born Cantonese under a red roof tile and a blue sky: San Francisco's Chinatown, 1950. Life in the red, and the hope of my parents in the blue. These facts alone compelled me to write." He received his B.A. from San Francisco State College and his M.F.A. from UCLA School of Film and Television. His work has been anthologized in *Asian American Authors* (Houghton Mifflin, 1971) and *Aiiieee! An Anthology of Asian American Writers* (Howard University Press, 1974). Since 1977, he has served as editor of UCLA's *Amerasia Journal.* He was the editor of *Moving the Image: Independent Asian Pacific American Media Arts* (Visual Communications and UCLA, 1991). His video documentaries include *Morning Begins Here* (1985) and *Why is Preparing Fish a Political Act? The Poetry of Janice Mirikitani* (1990).

Aerogrammes

(after a trip to Sunwui county—
Guangdong, China—1984)

Par avion
via airmail
hung-kung:
Only after I returned
to L.A. did China
collapse in my hand—
folded, sealed,
glued & stamped
westward.

I did not ask to be followed.
But someone's village childhood,
spent among the palmettos
pigs & orange groves
of the Pearl River delta
caught up with me
generations later.

Now, five blue and red
striped aerogrammes
corner my desk
airmail-stickered
in French, English & Chinese
addressing my journey
to Sunwui.

In Canton city
The words of the woman cadre
dart past my ears:
"Don't get your relatives Marlboros
why spoil them!

Local cigarettes are good enough—
and good for the economy!"
How 'bout a chicken?
I ask.
"Wait and see—
you may not like
your country cousins!"
I slip four cartons—
two American brand—
& two Chinese
into my bag
anyway.

Harvest
is over by December.
Along the pockmarked roads,
men knee-deep in winter mud
fill ditches
repair dikes.
Traffic holds us up—
I give the cadre
a piece of mind:
"When I was young
in America, we believed
in Mao, revolution,
socialism. Now China
travels the capitalist road—
what should we believe?"
She laughs.
"We never had ships
searching for spices or gold,
or far-flung empires built on slaves.
But a little capitalism today
is a good tonic
to cure feudal ideas!"
She sips a Coca-Cola
I buy at the roadside stand.
Traffic unsnarls—

we reach Sunwui
where she leaves me
to a local fellow
from the village clan.

In the clan hall
around a wooden table
the elders tug
at stray whiskers
in thought.
From my pocket,
I fetch
a black & white photo
of my father from World War II.
"Does anyone here remember this man?"
They pick at the image
like a scab off memory
narrow their vision
down to the eye,
recap their stories
down to the tooth.

No, no; yes, yes.
forward & backward
they lead me
through alleyways
smelling of
fish & oranges
to a small house.
I open the door—
my father stares down
from a wartime portrait
on the wall.
I cannot deny the relation
when all the children
in the room
suddenly chime "uncle."

AEROGRAMME 1: Los Angeles

I confess
I did not open the first letter
for a week.
Not that I feared using a dictionary
but the eight-legged ideograms
were like crabs
scuttling after my past.

"Your cousins and nephews
were happy to scatter wine
with you
over the ancestral hillside. . . ."
the letter began.
(I see
them hack away
the green thicket
clearing a path
to bring gravestone markers
to light.
They hadn't climbed
here in months, or more).

Later
Between spats
at tin spittoons
they splatter me
with questions.
"How old are you?
Are you married?
How many sons
did your father have?
Are they married?"
They press
bags of dried orange peel
at me
I answer with wine,
cigarettes & money.

AEROGRAMME 2.

"Your relatives
in Sunwui county
wish good health to you,
to your mother & brother.
By the way
you know that
free enterprise
is alive & well
in China, indeed
we would like
to open
a dry goods shop
but we lack capital.
Send as much as you can spare."

They did not name a figure
leaving it to my guilt or grace.
But I admitted none
for once, in Sunwui city
the county capital
I saw a photo exhibit
of toothy Chinese
from Indonesia,
Canada, Singapore,
San Francisco.

They had invested dollars
in a primary school here,
a textile factory there—
but I had no coined
compatriotism
to tender.

Instead
I xeroxed a photo
of my old uncle
the one in the polaroid
wearing the hand-me-down jacket,
earmuffs, and torn green sneakers.
"Buy him and auntie
winter coats
and divide the rest of the money,"
I wrote, alongside
the good side of his face
that was not twisted by stroke.

He looks me straight
in the eye
beyond a cold morning
to a day
right after the War.
"In 1947," he says
"I was sixteen.
Standing by the riverbank
I waited patiently
for the ferry
to come upstream
carrying U.N. rations
& your father.
He was the first
from California
to step upon village soil
after the Japanese
laid down their guns.
He came, ate, sprinkled
American scotch & water
on the gravestones
& left.
Months later, he
sent us that picture
of himself in a G.I. uniform—
We never heard from him again."

I blame the cold war.
My uncle nods.
And when I tell him that father
has just died
he shakes his head
without surprise.

AEROGRAMME 3.

"Greetings
from the factory cooperative
in Sunwui City.
The family"
my nephew began,
"hopes to buy a government condominium
Please send five thousand dollars—U.S.
Tomorrow."

I took it in stride.
Checked the horoscope
in the *L.A. Times*
but Virgo refused
to speculate that far.
Consulted close friends.
The ones from China said:
"Send the money."
The ones from America said:
"Crazy, man."

I had split vision.
In my left eye—
a new village house
yellow tiles, concrete block walls
a slab floor without cracks.
Running water, interior pipes
& lightbulbs
electrifying every room.

In my right eye—
a Los Angeles barrio
red spanish tiles aglow
over a stucco bungalow
leaning from the last earthquake,
palm trees, taco trucks
smoggy orange sunsets—
At thirty times the price
of a condo in Canton.
I winced.
Waited.
Waivered.
Calculated
mortgage points
exchange rates:
Four U.S. dollars
to one Chinese.

Procrastination sped me
to the new year
forced open my hand.
I telexed money from L.A. Chinatown,
to Hong Kong, to Canton,
to Sunwui village.
A token, less
than what they wanted
after finding that
they stood second, or third
on the family tree—
not in direct line
from grandfather, but
offshoots
concocted further back.

AEROGRAMME 4.

"Dear cousin in Los Angeles
We pen this letter
on behalf of your aunt
who went with us
to sweep family graves
again.
We chopped our way
thru last year's branches
& wondered when
you would return.

For, as fate had it
as she climbed down the hill
Auntie met
a young lass,
still single
supple as a willow.
It's time to start a family
agreed?"

Struck by the thought
I slid
into my '71 Ford Maverick
and cruised down Hollywood Boulevard.
Hookers—of both sexes
were walking nowhere
squinting
against the sun
at four in the afternoon.

AEROGRAMME 5.

Differed from the rest.
The writing quicker.
"Sir
I know it's bold
of me to write you.
I'll be twenty-two this year.
Didn't your auntie tell you
we met on the mountain?
I apologize
for my lack of schooling
I'm a country girl.
But I'm healthy
and you're of age.
If you want to see
me the next time
you return
please answer
my letter."

On the upper left corner
a two-inch photo
of a ten-story hotel
topped by a revolving restaurant
above
the palmettos
& orange groves
caught my eye.
Where was her face?

This is the last aerogramme
I've received so far.
I never showed them
to anyone
though
upon my return
I had pressed
the polaroids, like leaves
into an album.

"They look like
real Chinese
peasants, don't they!"
my mother said.
"You should see
Sunwui one day,"
I told my brother.
"Someday," he said.

Flattened and forgotten
the aerogrammes
lost their edge
until yesterday
when the *New York Times*
reported that
the People's Republic—
through a U.S. Chinese businessman—
planned to export
Chinese workers
to harvest American farms.
This is what he said:
"exporting workers
is like exporting oil—
or silk slippers."
But what we need now is bodies—
he meant to say.

His words hit dirt
reviving my suspicions.
Maybe matters
like aerogrammes,
family reunions,
gravesweeping,
and revolving restaurants
rising from the delta mud—
were just
concessions for export—
like oil or silk slippers.

Only
after I returned
from China
did the idea collapse
in my head:
I swore off
grimy ancestral markers—
I wrote off
filial piety
as useless;
a fallen branch.

Yet
as keenly
as the blade
of the letter opener
that falls upon my hand
I await the arrival
of the next
immutable
aerogramme.

Wing Tek Lum

Wing Tek Lum's first collection of poetry, *Expounding the Doubtful Points,* was published by Bamboo Ridge Press in 1987.

A Picture of My Mother's Family

At a summer home in Ningpo, near Shanghai,
your family (circa 1915) poses on the stone floor entryway
between the rise of steps and the wood front door.
Four girls are spread about the parents,
who are seated. All are in warm clothing,
finely dressed. It is perhaps morning, the coolness
captured now in such clear light: they seem, somehow,
more illumined by beams emanating from the moon.

On the right, Ming, the second-born, my living aunt,
has on a dark wool dress and brocaded top of silk
that does not cover her sleeves. She tiptoes slightly,
for she leans to one side on her hidden right arm
bracing, it would seem, on the edge of her father's chair.
Her face—cocked to her right in front of his chest—
is plump. The supple mouth I recognize
smiles downward, frowning: sad and shy
in her own young world. This photograph is hers;
last year she gave it to me in remembrance of you.

My grandfather is seated on white upholstery,
upright, balding and in black, even to his bow tie.
The shine on his shoes reflects into the camera
as he looks on, disregarding the cluster of children,
towards his right faraway. I imagine a dark rose
has caught his proud eye, though I do not know
if such flowers have ever grown there.
The grain of the picture reveals his fine hands,
as if all were focused upon them alone.
The fingers are brown and slender, recalling
that he was a doctor, and that these are doctor's hands.
Gnarled roots, they had grown as pale as his beard
and clothes, when we saw him—I at the age of five
in Hong Kong, after he was allowed in for the last time.

Holding his right hand in her small clasp,
her arm snuggled against his thigh, the third daughter
(maybe three) glances with eyebrows raised
somewhere in the direction of her father's gaze.
Her stance is as wide as her padded skirt, disclosing
beneath a small foot balancing on its outer side.
I guess that her silk top is red, a color
of wide cherries. The shortest in the picture,
she stands dwarfed by the shadows looming behind her.
Funny, but I don't even know her name; I think
she was the one, you said, who never reached her teens.

Lucy, the youngest sister, leans forward
on her mother's lap: squirming, I assume,
for her left arm is in a blur, swinging,
her mouth opened round, voicing her discomfort.
She is all white in a doll's bonnet and long dress,
as if she were attending her own wedding.
More likely, it's her birthday . . .
She never married, moved to Chicago near Ming.
At forty, she visited our home, skinny and sallow
from cancer. Soon after, picking me up
from school, you told me, "she just passed away."

Caught at that moment, your mother looks into the lens,
while restraining her daughter: her hands in front
encircling the waist. She wears a wan smile,
almost serene. Partly it's because of her face,
which seems flat. I can discern no part of her nose,
except for the line of a shadow beneath her nostrils.
Her trousers are nearly covered by the spread
of Lucy's dress. I notice that wrinkles have begun
to set under her eyes; they make her appear
out of focus, like crying. I muse about
whether her feet were bound. A pastor's daughter,
she died young. My grandfather remarried.

The one on the left end, you are as tall
as your parents are when seated. With black boots on
you balance playfully on the balls of your feet,
a bit pigeon-toed. For you, the oldest,
your mother has combed all your hair back tightly
about your head; you wear to one side a paper flower:
white, to match your own long blouse and pants.
Although proper, I suppose, the sleeves
and the trouser legs are cut three-quarters length,
as if you had already outgrown these clothes.
Forearms exposed, I can see a thin bracelet
around each wrist. With your flat nose
and flower, I almost think you are a small clown.
Your mouth closed, you keep smiling straight at me.

Urban Love Songs

after Tzu Yeh

You stop to watch the Mandarin ducks.
The rest of us continue on to the flamingo lagoon.
I would like to ask what attracts you to them.
But my feet keep walking, I don't look back.

. . .

From a piece of cloth I cut out a heart.
In the laundromat it is washed and dried.
I can spend whole hours watching it toss and tumble.
I wonder if you feel the same way as I.

. . .

I wave as you enter; you take your seat smiling.
This same coffee shop now feels crowded.
We whisper to each other:
all eyes have noticed something's changed.

. . .

I've bought a new phone and an answering machine
because I know you will be calling.
Here's the number, which only you will have.
I plan to change the tape every hour on the hour.

. . .

Our friends are laughing.
They say we sit so close in your old Buick
it has become second nature for me
to exit on the same side as you.

. . .

Pinocchio's back!
Let's relive that night at the drive-in
when I whispered that his nose was giving me ideas
and you got into my pants for the first time.

. . .

You drop the laundry off going to work.
I bring the bag back when I come home.
Neatly folded, your underthings are left on the bed
—I wish to respect certain cabinets as yours.

. . .

You shut the window rushing to your covers
complaining of the cold night.
I need fresh air, but am willing to compromise.
Let's just pull up the sash halfway, okay?

. . .

We hunt for photos in my parents' storeroom.
Look how young I was and full of dreams.
On the way out you brush against a cobweb.
Your flailing arms make me afraid.

. . .

A firetruck screams through my heart.
Douse the flames! Douse the flames!
I awake to find my pillow soaked with sweat.
For a moment I thought it was my tears.

    . . .

You've stacked your boxes neatly by the door.
I find atop one Chinese poems I had bought for us.
Quietly I take the book out.
I resolve to tell you this after you have moved.

    . . .

For my clogged sink I called a plumber.
When my cat got ill I took her to the vet.
My heart is broken
—I will not ask you to come to mend me.

    . . .

Last night you made me so mad.
I've resolved never ever to speak to you again.
I regret having to put my foot down so.
I'm sending you a telegram to let you know.

    . . .

One friend I know cut her hair short.
Another shaved his beard without regrets.
I would walk this city naked and bald
if ever I thought I could be free of you.

    . . .

After you, I took up jogging.
I wore through my running shoes in no time.
One night I chucked them down into the trash chute.
See how trim I am these days!

. . .

Once I bought a single chrysanthemum on a stem.
We watched it blossom, red and full.
Those times now bring a smile to me
finding its brown petals as I sweep the floor.

Riding the North Point Ferry

Wrinkles: like
valleys etched by glaciers
lumbering coarse
and deliberate, random
traces pointing to
that vast, dark sea. The skin
is an ochre
of old corn, with
splotches of
burnt embers from a summer
of mountain fires.
The brown
from a lifetime of tea or
tobacco or both
has stained her
uneven teeth. Ears and nose
are small, pudgy,
and on each
lobe a little knob of gold
tacked on.
She sits with one
leg raised, tucked
into her body, the heel
supported by
the seat, her arm
resting on her
knee—unladylike to be
sure, though
in her black garments
a relaxed pose. I glance at
her eyes, mottled
now with a chicken-fat
yellow in the

pupils, gazing out at the harbor,
the neon lights beckoning
from the Kowloon
shore.

            Where
was I prepared for this
face? Not
from the land of
my birth, with our museums,
glass cases filled
with the porcelain of ancient
dynasties, restaurateurs (cheeks
of cupidity)
proffering hot
and sour delights, our bookstores
extolling Shangri-las in
paperback—all to deny
our scrutable
lives. We believe
that somewhere in the world our
exotica is real. Images
of all fairy tale
maidens: clear-eyed yet
coy, hair pure
as silk, skin like jade,
the small hands so clever and
refined—and when
held in my own, how
warm, yielding to the touch!
They are
fiction: like the wind-blown
waves across this
ferry's bow, an inconstant
surface of
reflection, glittering, oblivious
to the swollen
depths below.

I know
that outward appearances are
no judge for
virtue within. And
even this old
woman, combing her loosed
hair at dawn,
must sometimes wonder
at that mirrored form, peering
from those eyes. Does
she recognize
that dark glow as
her own? We meet so many
dreams, so many tales
of woe. Which
ones are true? Which ones
our alibis? So hard to
choose.

My grandparents
I recall sailed by
sea to settle in
that place we now call home.
I have crossed that
ocean too, flying this time
with the sun,
searching for a vision
for my own. The deck rocks gently.
By chance I find
myself beside this woman
on this crowded
boat: she is
for me reason enough to
have come here.

Janice Mirikitani

George T. Kruse

   Janice Mirikitani, a Sansei, is recognized as a poet,
choreographer, administrator, teacher, and community or-
ganizer/activist. Currently, she is President of the Glide
Corporation, a nonprofit entity operating in the Bay Area,
and Program Director of the Glide Church/Urban Center.
She has edited numerous anthologies including *AION Mag-
azine, Third World Women,* and *Time to Greez! Incantations
from the Third World.* She served as Project Director and
Editor of *AYUMI,* a Japanese American anthology span-
ning four generations. She is coeditor of *Making Waves,* an
Asian Women's anthology sponsored by Asian Women
United. She has published two books of poetry and prose,
Awake in the River (Isthmus Press, 1978) and *Shedding Silence*
(Celestial Arts Publishing, 1987).

Soul Food

For Cecil

We prepare
the meal together.
I complain,
hurt, reduced to fury
again by their
subtle insults
insinuations
because I am married to you.
Impossible autonomy, no mind
of my own.

You like your fish
crisp, coated with cornmeal,
fried deep,
sliced mangos to sweeten
the tang of lemons.
My fish is raw,
on shredded lettuce,
lemon slices thin as skin,
wasabe burning like green fire.
You bake the cornbread flat
and dip it in
the thick soup
I've brewed from
turkey carcass, rice gruel,
sesame oil and chervil.

We laugh over watermelon
and bubbling cobbler.

You say,
there are few men
who can stand
to have a woman equal,
upright.

This meal,
unsurpassed.

The Fisherman

Ojichan was a fisherman/farmer
more a fisherman,
cleaning his bait
winding his line,
the smell of sardines
seeping from his sea-cracked hands.
The muscles of his face spoke
but his tongue silent
except for syllables
of survival

         sake

         oi ocha

         kata o momu

and obachan would
knead the strong knots
on his shoulders.
Only when he put on his boots
and left the house for China Lake
pipe cocked in his mouth
a certain way,
there seemed a light
from his straightened frame
eyes noisy,
muscles in a little dance.
And when he came home,
laughing as he fished his catch
from the depths of his box,
gloated that his old friend
Kinjo caught only one,
and set the stiff rainbow
pearled fish
out for the women to scale,
wide mouths gaping

surprised eyes encorpsing
the room.
Many nights
over sake
making guttural sounds
with Kinjo,
the light from him was brighter.
                    That winter
China Lake was
cold, winds shaped water
into hands, fingers
clawed the shore.
No one else would go
but Kinjo
rocking years and pride
rowed out with his son.
The boat turned
like a small fish
The old man
went down
water freezing in his bones.
His son reached for him,
dived two times
did not come up again.
The people
stood on the dock
and looked.
                    I think it hurt Ojichan
deeply
Kinjo fished from China Lake.
                    After,
he would sit
looking into the sun,
body dimmed
muscles knotted
eyes silent.
He wore his loss like his heavy boots,
legs moving

in slow underwater motion
when he learned how they
stood and looked
and did nothing.

Shadow in Stone

Journey to Hiroshima, Japan
International Peace Conference, 1984

We wander in the stifling heat
of August.
Hiroshima,
your museum, peace park,
paper cranes rustling whispers
of hei-wa   *peace*
Burning incense
throbbing with white chrysanthemums,
plum blossoms, mounds
of soundless bones.
Hiroshima
how you rise up
in relentless waves of heat.
I come to you late,
when the weather bludgeons, blisters.
       I put my mouth
on your burning sky
on the lips of your murmuring river.
Motoyasu, river of the dead.

    The river speaks:
        I received the bodies
        leaping into my wet arms
        their flesh in flame, and the flies
        that followed
        maggots in the bloated sightless waste,
        skin rotting like wet leaves.
        My rhythm stifled, my movement stilled.

Motoyasu cries with rituals,
bearing a thousand flickering candles
in floating lanterns of yellow, red, blue
to remember the suffering.
I light a lantern for grandmother's sister
whom they never found amidst the ashes
of your cremation.
She floats beside the other souls
as we gather, filling water
in the cups of our hands,
pouring it back into the thirsty mouths
of ghosts, stretching parched throats.

The heat presses like many hands.
I seek solace in the stone
with human shadow burned into its face.
      I want to put my mouth to it
to the shoulders of that body,
my tongue to wet its dusty heart.

      I ask the stone to speak:
         When I looked up,
         I did not see the sun
         a kind friend who has gently pulled
         my rice plants skyward.
         I worried in that moment
         if my child would find shade
         in this unbearable heat
         that melts my eyes.
         No, I did not see the sun.
         I saw what today
         mankind has created
         and I layed my body
         into this cool stone,
         my merciful resting place.

Museum of ruins.
The heat wrings our bodies
with its many fingers.
photographs remind us of a holocaust
and imagination stumbles, beaten, aghast.
        I want to put my mouth
against these ruins, the distorted teacup,
crippled iron,
melted coins,
a disfigured bowl.

        I ask the bowl to speak:
            The old man
            held his daughter,
            rocking her in his lap,
            day after day after
            that terrible day,
            she weak from radiation
            could not lift this bowl.
            Her face once bright like our sunset
            now white as ash,
            could not part her lips
            as he tried to spoon okayu from this bowl
            droplet by droplet
            into the crack of her mouth,
            the watered rice with umeboshi
            which he would chew to feed her.
            He did not know
            when she stopped breathing
            as he put his mouth to hers
            gently to pass food.
            He rocked her still body
            watching the red sunset
            burning its fiery farewell.

Hiroshima, rising up.
I come here late
when the weather sucks at us.
               I want to put my mouth
to the air, its many fingers of heat,
lick the twisted lips
of a disfigured bowl,
the burned and dusty heart of shadow in stone,
put my mouth to the tongues
of a river,
its rhythms, its living water
weeping on the sides of lanterns,
each floating flame, a flickering
voice murmuring
over and over
as I put my mouth
to echo
over and over
never again.

James Masao Mitsui

James Masao Mitsui was born in 1940 in Skykomish, Washington. He received a B.A. in education from Eastern Washington State University in 1963 and both his B.A. ('73) and M.A. ('75) in English from the University of Washington. For twenty-six years, he has been a high school English teacher, and in 1976, he was the recipient of an NEA Fellowship. His books include *Journal of the Sun* (Copper Canyon Press, 1974), *Crossing the Phantom River* (Graywolf Press, 1978), and *After the Long Train* (The Beiler Press, 1986).

Destination: Tule Lake Relocation Center, May 20, 1942

She had raised the window
higher

than her head; then
paused

to lift wire spectacles,
wiping

sight back with a wrinkled
hand-

kerchief. She wanted to watch
the old

place until the train's passing
erased

the tarpaper walls and tin roof;
she had

been able to carry away
so little.

The fingers of her left
hand

worried two strings
attached

to a baggage tag
flapping

from her
lapel.

Photograph of a Child, Japanese-American Evacuation, Bainbridge Island, Washington, March 30, 1942

The soft sound of his steps on the pier
is obscured by the heavy footfall

of the adults, rippling the planked deck.
One hand reaches above his head

to wrap around father's ring finger;
the other clutches a balsa model

of a U.S. fighter plane, held
upside down against his chest.

He is the only one who uses this time
to peer between the cracks at his feet,

trying to see the shiny ribs of water,
imagine a monstrous flounder hugging

the sediment, both eyes staring
from the top of its flat head.

Picture of a Japanese Farmer, Woodland, California, May 20, 1942

His waiting becomes a time to hear thoughts, the sound
of unseen sparrows, the glance for any movement
from a road on the other side of dark eyes.
It is the tossing down of a cigarette,
the quiet imprint of a twisting foot.

Behind him a butcher paper sign on a mailbox
sells what will be awkward tomorrow. Feet in black
Sunday shoes are stable as the block of wood on end
used for a seat. Elbows on knees, he looks hard
at the packed earth. A cigarette gone out
waits between fingers like an artist's brush.
Willows drift sap in their shadows, coating the man,
the ground and the top half of a discarded oil drum
on its side. The bottom has no viscous coat.
Dust will not adhere for this plain reason.

Nisei: Second Generation Japanese-American

They grow over the Yangtze, the plum rains
grow over water that drops
gently to the wideness of the East China sea.
Farmers in Kyushu are caught by the floating clouds,
caught square in the middle of their fields,
squinting to see who it is
standing there on the dirt bank, the mud
in the soft rain, soft as the leading edge of a cloud.

I write this on a day that has twisted away
from doubt. Happy to be here
still I have a place on that gray continent,
far home of my grandfathers
those figures I never saw through the haze
of mountains except in picture. Photographs
yellow and brown as old newsprint,
smudges of thought, of fingers and skin.
Time to realize the importance of rain.
Rain on the ground,
and rain still falling.

Katori Maru, October 1920

Two weeks across a strange sea,
big waves, the ship
spilling its toilets.
People sick of the ocean
run from bulkhead to bulkhead,
trying to keep their balance
on the slick iron deck.

My mother asks herself in Japanese
why her oldest sister had to die,
why now she must marry the stranger
who speaks Japanese & English
and swears with the crew.
She thinks back to Nagano-ken,
pictures her mother
cracking a brown egg
over a bowl of rice
while her father washes raw soil
from his thick hands.
Today she could trade her future
for the bottom of the ocean.

Waves, floating waves,
rise above the railing,
drift out of sight. Vancouver Island
is a memory of home, hills
soft & green as crushed velvet.

In Tacoma, Minoru buys
Western clothes: a pink taffeta dress
full of pleats, wide-brimmed hat,
white gloves, a leather handbag
and awkward high heels.

No more flowered silk,
obi sash and getas.
He brings out a used coat from the closet,
thick maroon wool, brown fur collar.
It is too full in the shoulders,
the size & color
fit her sister.
But for now she accepts it.
The rain feels heavy
on the gray sidewalks of America.

At Bon Odori

The drumbeat is constant as surf
after days of ocean. It becomes
a heartbeat. The footwork of the drummer,
the way each swing has meaning
and is sure, reminds me of father
just before retiring. Drunk on payday night,
he'd sing a Japanese song on our front porch
that meant nothing to me
surrounded by a small town, sagebrush
and hills that stayed out of the way
of a crick.

Clapping hands between each pause
of thumping foot, father wove
130 pounds of rhythm with biceps
I always admired. That's what swinging
a pick or sledge-hammer could do.
Thirteen-years-old, I'd come up
between the ritual of his dance,
wrap growing arms around his hard chest,
capturing his darker arms
and lift in a half-circle, carrying him
back inside, out of the light
that took the shape of our front door
fallen down. Once inside
he'd challenge me to some judo,
telling me the story
I had heard more than anyone in the family.

Not the oldest son, at 16, he left the farm
in Nagano-Ken, gone to Tokyo
and had been tossed out of a club
that taught self-defense.
Right into the street, he'd laugh,
just like this, as I held his still strong grip
and pulled him up off the floor
where I had tackled him, not understanding judo.
When you fall, he said, before you land,
hit the floor harder first
with your hand & arm. It won't hurt.

Because of My Father's Job

Spring hailstones would drive us
into the garage. I'd explain away
the smell of my father's tsukemono crock
with its rock-weight,
saying he needed his cabbage
like Popeye's spinach. I'd divert attention
to the moonsnail shell,
carried across the mountains from Puget Sound
by my sister. We'd shake off cobwebs,
listen to the dancing surf.

I still use the smell of cabbage,
like kelp & fishbone, as an anchor
although I have no memories of father
scooping butter clams
out of the gravel at Point-of-Arches
near Shi Shi Beach. Nothing
to connect him to the wind
on the headland at Strawberry Point,
the breakers unfolding a story
of poetry, edges & days
that don't always balance.

I have no memories of father
naming me
after Jimmy Osler of Skykomish,
who worked in the depot
and laughed so easily.
Who didn't change his friendship in '41.

I have copied the moustache
we shaved off my father once
when he was drunk. Last December
I sat at a motel kitchen table,
on the Oregon coast,
writing poems by candlelight.
My shadow fluttered on the walls & ceiling
as white waves
thundered & slid toward the cabin.
Turning to a mirror
I found his thick biceps
flexing themselves.
It doesn't matter now that he drank too much,
embarrassed the moon with his curses & songs.

David Mura

Rob Lee

David Mura is a Sansei, and was born in 1952. He
received his B.A. from Grinnell College, did graduate work
in English at the University of Minnesota, and received his
M.F.A. from Vermont College. He is the author of *After
We Lost Our Way* (Dutton, 1989), which won the National
Poetry Series Contest; *Turning Japanese: Memoirs of a Sansei*
(Atlantic Monthly Press, 1991; Anchor/Doubleday, 1992);
and *A Male Grief: Notes on Pornography and Addiction* (Milk-
weed Editions, 1987). His poems have appeared in *The
Nation, The New Republic, New England Review, Crazyhorse,*
and *The American Poetry Review*. He has received a US-Japan
Creative Artist Fellowship, an NEA Literature Fellowship,
two Bush Foundation Fellowships, a Loft-McKnight
Award, two Minnesota State Arts Board grants, a Pushcart
Prize, and a Discovery/*The Nation* Award. He lives in St.
Paul, Minnesota, with his wife, Susan Sencer, a pediatric
oncologist, and their daughter, Samantha.

The *Hibakusha's* Letter (1955)

Survivors of the atomic bomb were called hibakusha. *This name became associated with keloids, a whitish-yellow scar tissue, and later, with defects, disease, and disgrace.*

The fields, Teruko-san, are threshed. A good
Harvest. All week I've seen farmers with torches
Bend to earth, releasing fires. The winds
Sweep ash across the roads, dirty my laundry

Hung on the fence. Prayer drums, gongs, clap
In the streets, and now the village celebrates.
Last night Matsuo told me how he emptied
On a clump of rags beside the inn. Suddenly

The clump jumped up, groggy, wet, cursing.
Matsuo finished, bowed, offered him a drink.
This morning I shuffled out back to gossip
With my neighbor, an eighty-year-old woman

Who prances like a mouse about her garden.
While she jabbered Matsuo cut her firewood;
Sweat poured from the scars he no longer marks.
Later I opened my shrine to its brass Buddha,

And fruit flies scattered from the bowl of plums
I'd forgotten to change. Pulled from the rubble,
Burnt at the edges, my fiancé's picture
Crumbled in my fingers. I lit him incense.

Matsuo says we can't drag each corpse behind us
Like a shadow. The eye blinks, a world's gone,
And the slow shudder at our shoulders says
We won't be back. This year I've changed my diet:

I eat only rice, *utskemono, tofu.*
Sashimi sickens me, passion for raw meat.
Sister, remember how Mother strangled chickens?
She twirled them in the air by their necks

Like a boy with a slingshot. I'd watch in horror
Their bodies twitch, hung from her fist, and cry
That Buddha kept their karma in my stomach.
Like them we had no warning. Flames filled kimonos

With limbs of ash, and I wandered past
Smoldering trolleys away from the city.
Of course you're right. We can't even play beauty
Or the taste of steel quickens our mouths.

I can't conceive, and though Matsuo says
It doesn't matter, my empty belly haunts me:
Why call myself a woman, him a man,
If on our island only ghosts can gather?

And yet, I can't deny it. There are times,
Teruko, I am happy . . .
You say *hibakusha* should band together. Here
Fewer eyes shower us in shame. I wandered

Too far: My death flashed without, not within.
I can't come back. To beg the world's forgiveness
Gains so little, and monuments mean nothing.
I can't choose your way or even Matsuo's:

"Drink, Yoshiko, *sake*'s the one surgeon
Doesn't cost or cut." This evening, past fields black
And steaming, the pitch of night soil, I'll wander
Up foothills to the first volcanic springs.

After a wind from hell, the smell of burning
Now seems sweeter than flowers . . .

Gardens We Have Left

1

As Sam crumbles lumps of tofu on her tray,
I sizzle onions in oil, shoyu, rice wine,
add noodles, ginger, sugar, *shiitake;*

shoots of bamboo and chrysanthemum leaves.
Before the beef, veined with fat, thin as gauze,
I stir what for years I could not love.

(As a child, I shunned *mochi, futomaki,*
loved hot dogs, baseball, the GI John Wayne.
Now my *hashi* hauls up steaming *sukiyaki.*)

Later I take Sam out back, dressed in her *happi,*
and humming like my grandfather *sakura,*
think of a trip to Ise, her learning Japanese.

Pulling drooping petunias, scattering petals
like a cyclone, she starts trampling the garden.
Soon she's crumbling parsley, mint, basil,

vines blackened dry as ash; now she splatters
tomatoes, half-caved in, shriveling with rot.
If this were August, I'd shout and stop her,

but since it's autumn, the clouds burnished, cool,
I let it spill from her, some giggle caught
from you, how her spine stoops and curls

like yours as you weed, trowel or clip flowers.
The air darkens, milky galaxies pour over us.
As I pick her up, Sam points, "Star . . . star . . . star . . ."

Feeling her weight, I think how someone
someday will call her *gook,* as surely as
this taste of ginger breathing on my tongue;

how the other day at this wedding, you
were matron of honor, and the priest greeted
you: "Oh, I've heard so much about you.

You must have such a large heart, it's so
generous of you to adopt this child . . ."
Suddenly, I envision—why would I want to

see this?—a white sheet descending, mapping
the body of my father, his dark leathery face
almost blue, like a baby before the slap

that shuttles its howl out to the world.
The sheet washes him from sight, the way
surf sucks up footprints from the shore—

Who will tell our daughter about the dark
gardener's boy who swam the Venice surf,
who never returned to L.A. after the war?

A late moth, a few crickets. I hear you call
us, the skin on our bodies, warm at last.
A man holds his child, sees his father laid

out in the sleep of his death. The wind
brushes his face. And then, it's his child's hand.

2

Suppose I try to tell Sam of my grandfather,
his J-Town hotel, pool hall or nursery?
I know so little even of father's fatigue

at his dim-lit desk at INS, as he rested on
his typewriter, deadline approaching, the keys
leaving little circles of letters on his brow.

Neither he nor my mother talk of the past;
my childhood myths are Saturday's cartoons.
All my father recalls is a March marriage,

unfurling in a damp cold room, how the groom
believed in Shakespeare and the flag, in my mother
giggling amid a crowd of Nisei girls, the band

bopping out "Begin the Beguine." It was 1950,
after the camps, the war, all the West Coast hysteria
lost in yellowed headlines no one retrieved.

Yesterday, at the campus grill with my blond, blue-
eyed students, over burgers and fries, Gordon
Hirabayashi spoke of refusing the '42 curfew,

how he wandered all night the Seattle streets.
Finally, foot-weary, hackled, he slapped open
the Police Station doors, strode to the desk,

and ordered they arrest him in his civil protest.
For months he would pace his cell, roaches
like sparks scattering from his steps,

and after countless prayers to his Quaker God,
he stood before the Court and uttered a "no"
they refused to hear. Sent to camp without a ticket,

whistling in the dark, he thumbed his way there,
wild hares scattering across the white-lined asphalt,
the Dipper spilling overhead its cup of stars . . .

With wire-rimmed glasses, and hair softly greying,
looking almost a double of my father,
he reached into that era, held it before me

pulsing like a vein. And I somehow knew:
Had *he* been my father, had my father spoke once
like this, I would not be dabbing *shoyu*

from the chin of our *happa*-eyed daughter;
your Pilgrim face could not have compelled me
in quite the same way. Love, did my desire

sprout where history died? It's all speculation.
We are together, My father is alive.

3

Of course, it's an old tune—people migrating
across a river, a mountain, an ocean;
embarking, disembarking, leaving luggage,

customs, finding homes, lovers, children . . .
Who cares about past gardens, relocations, or race?
You and Sam take a bath; I wash dishes.

And the Buddha dies nightly on the road.
Perhaps I've learned to say: This is my home,
this yard where squirrels forage pine cones,

popcorn and pumpkin seeds from our garbage,
where our daughter's fears are measured
in sparrows, shadows, the mongrel next door

banging his cage. Where nightly I prepare
neither for angels or some Virgil
but the bottle and teddy bear and lullabye books.

So why do I insist on telling you this tale?
In 1944, set free with a sharp jolt, like lightning
loosed from a cloud, my father stood

outside those gates in Jerome, waving
back at his mother and father, their faces
sectioned by wires, like pieces of

a puzzle or invisible windows. Dust
puffed up a ridge where a bus reared
into view, and the young man, impatient,

stepped out of memory and into a world
without obligations or magic, prosaic
as that campus in Kalamazoo, where he

would walk beside white coeds and the young boys
like him, breathing in a fragrance of
burning leaves, perfume and war.

Soon the landscape darkens so early,
the last sun skimming Arkansas hills,
swamp rot and mist drifting where

bullfrogs and crickets unsettle the night,
and an owl houses in his sight something
scurrying below. In the barracks, beside

the beds, now empty (he is the next to
last child to leave), *otoo-san* and *okaa-san*
fall into each other's frail limbs, listen

to the rain plop through cracks in the roof,
the storm overhead marking their loss.
Three hundred miles away, their son

looks out the window, a cigarette
glowing before him in the dark. His face
looks lonelier than I have ever seen it.

And I see now he too is like a window
I have gazed through all my life. How
little I have gazed at him in wonder.

This too, like Sam, is my hymn to America.

4

There are years the earth devours. What is it father
says of the camps? "In L.A. each day I'd sweat
and shove a mower for my father

across the lawns in Beverly Hills. During the war,
after school, I played baseball." Hey, Buddhahead,
how do you link amnesia with desire?

At fourteen, after school in my room in Oak Park,
I traced fashion ads from papers, stripping
white models, sketching in nipples, pubic hair.

Why did I start that gallery of obscene despair?
Out of that garden where the serpent hisses,
years ago, my great-grandmother carved

daikon to the bulbous head of a penis,
paraded to the shrine with daikon members
held erect by the Shingu women, their clogs

wobbling through the mud: It was harvest,
in the fields fires burned stubble to ash.
And the mountain gods whispered through cedars.

And the women sang, and later roasted and ate
those members, their teeth crooked and black.
—Suppose I had loved a woman like that?

Would I still be singing to Sam of wishing stars,
the blackbird that flings its caw from the eaves,
of ghosts and fairies, of walking amid flowers

just above the underworld, its demon caves?
And will she know I lived there once, and sat
in dark booths where the images displayed

whiteness as paradise made flesh, a bar where
nothing expires but consciousness spliced
in x-rated loops; come cry, scotch, and shudder,

dope, poppers, bodies that fueled my racial rage?
(So often, standing at the door, mumbling casually,
"I'm going to the store," I'd watch you gaze

up from your studies, and for a second, sigh—
Hours later, I'd return, the lie still inside . . .)

5

So often I go back to a greenhouse of roses,
each thorn bearing a droplet, each droplet
a sphere where you could spy a rose

or a spy according to your skin. How does
that song end? After grandmother's death,
after returning to the rebuilt rubble of Tokyo,

grandfather was buried somewhere on Koya-san,
amid graves of samurai, presidents of *kaisha*,
carpenters, priests, merchants and courtesans.

Years later, when my aunt traveled to find his grave,
she searched for hours amid century old stones.
Near evening, on the moss-heavy path,

in the cedar shadows, she broke into tears
at ashes irrevocably gone. Is this our legacy?
The past lies in this vase. The vase disappears.

I will say it now: In that soft-silted carbon,
the burnt flecks of bone no Nikkei can find,
what's missing is a history, a man, a nation.

In the months after Pearl, as headlines declare
Nips on the coast nurture fifth columns,
cajoling Gen. Dewitt, his military nightmares,

is a JACL Nisei who knows no Japanese,
who swears by Saturday reels of Erroll Flynn
shooting savages for God, flag and Gary Owen.

(This Moses foresees in the sands of Anzio,
in shrapnel some Nisei will bleed at the Bulge,
the pride of purple hearts, PR, and heroes.)

At panel after panel, he *asks* the authorities
to isolate Issei (in private suggests they brand them);
proposes internment to prove our loyalty,

and proclaims in some senator's ear
how unfamiliar he is with Buddha, how Christ
and the flag have made his accent disappear.

And later, in the camps, as JACL'ers
finger No-No's, kibei and other resisters,
and even suggest marrying out their sisters . . .

Suddenly I think of your face, our daughter's—
Where did I learn to love? Are these my fathers?

6

Who pardons fathers now and so long ago?
Or blesses my digging like a worm the gardens
of Shingu and Jerome and Little Tokyo?

Some Masaoka, some Hirabayashi,
some grandmother's daughter named Ruth,
who hated for years the sight of any Japanese;

the soldiers who left their breath and blood
foaming and swirling in the Anzio tide
or in dark stretches of some German wood,

or the ones who, like my uncle, returned
to signs proclaiming as before, "No Japs served,"
loud as the notices that kept them interned;

those that served and those who would not serve,
whose speeches are written out of the books,
some Frank Emi, a black belt grocer,

or Omura, the reporter, whose pages were turned
over to authorities for the higher good—
not one of them can yield those years again.

Why bring them to bear on this song, our daughter,
the vines she tramples and the fists of flowers
she sprinkles on the lawn? Though I'm her father,

I know how little can pass down to a child.
(You know how my father and I fought those years
I declared like a boy that I would not kill,

and had no quarrel with the slant-eyed Cong.
We did not speak of it for years. The years are gone.
And my father is a stranger. Who loves his son.)

Dear, although I've come now to thirty-nine,
and share with you this child who bears your nose,
my eyes, and what is neither yours nor mine,

all I can offer her are these rumors and stories,
this legacy halved or doubled as the case may be.

7

Tonight as you breathe beside me,
I think of how your body rolled beneath mine
moments ago, plunging over me

as I sank deeper, past the image of our daughter,
petunia in her fist, the aroma of *sukiyaki,*
Coltrane and love sounds like a sirocco in our ears.

Perhaps something is endlessly tracing
inside me memories trapped and released
in the body, like the roses that replaced

daikon in my grandfather's soil, shot
with steam as the L.A. sun streamed through
a dozen greenhouse panes. How it should plot

in heaven I don't know; our garden is terrestrial,
owned by imagination, and in it our daughter
skitters up to my father, flings her arms at his knees

while behind him, in the shadow of a cedar,
as the temple bells echo into evening,
ojii-san, obaa-san clap their hands together,

and bow their heads . . .—Think of all
the devourings of flesh, the way a babe
suckles, nuzzling the nipple with gummy jaws,

or how some Mifune samurai slouches to his *hashi*;
how our daughter nibbles pea pods, grasses, beans,
or the earth swallows her dead, sanding

flesh, leaves, bones; peeling hair, eyelids,
bark, bugs and bacteria searing through soil.
What do I find here in the gaze of a toddler,

this ancestral food, the lines my father once cast
in the L.A. surf, or those I paste to this page?
When you hold a great sorrow, it lasts

almost too long. And then it lasts some more.
But the same is true also of a great joy.
In the island of light we make with our bodies,

in the lullabyes where our daughter sleeps,
we open a picture book, and the images are
for the first time. Once I lost something

of great value. And then I sought it.
Everything changed then. Everything changed.

Cathy Song

Andrea Song Gelber

Cathy Song, born in 1955 and raised in Honolulu, Hawaii, holds degrees from Wellesley College and Boston University. She is the author of *Picture Bride* (Yale, 1983), which won the Yale Series of Younger Poets Award in 1982 and was nominated for the National Book Critics Circle Award. Her second book, *Frameless Windows, Squares of Light,* appeared from W.W. Norton in 1991. Her poetry has been widely anthologized in various collections including *The Morrow Anthology of Younger American Poets, The Heath Anthology of American Literature,* and *The Norton Anthology of Modern Poetry.* She lives and teaches in Honolulu.

Easter: Wahiawa, 1959

1

The rain stopped for one afternoon.
Father brought out
his movie camera and for a few hours
we were all together
under a thin film
that separated the rain showers
from that part of the earth
like a hammock
held loosely by clothespins.

Grandmother took the opportunity
to hang the laundry
and Mother and my aunts
filed out of the house
in pedal pushers and poodle cuts,
carrying the blue washed eggs.

Grandfather kept the children
penned in on the porch,
clucking at us in his broken English
whenever we tried to peek
around him. There were bread crumbs
stuck to his blue gray whiskers.

I looked from him to the sky,
a membrane of egg whites
straining under the weight
of the storm that threatened
to break.

We burst loose from Grandfather
when the mothers returned
from planting the eggs
around the soggy yard.
He followed us,
walking with stiff but sturdy legs.
We dashed and disappeared
into bushes,
searching for the treasures;
the hard-boiled eggs
which Grandmother had been simmering
in vinegar and blue color all morning.

2

When Grandfather was a young boy
in Korea,
it was a long walk
to the riverbank,
where, if he were lucky,
a quail egg or two
would gleam from the mud
like gigantic pearls.
He could never eat enough
of them.

It was another long walk
through the sugarcane fields
of Hawaii,
where he worked for eighteen years,
cutting the sweet stalks
with a machete. His right arm
grew disproportionately large
to the rest of his body.
He could hold three
grandchildren in that arm.

I want to think
that each stalk that fell
brought him closer
to a clearing,
to that palpable field
where from the porch
to the gardenia hedge
that day he was enclosed
by his grandchildren,
scrambling around him,
for whom he could at last buy
cratefuls of oranges,
basketfuls of sky blue eggs.

I found three that afternoon.
By evening, it was raining hard.
Grandfather and I skipped supper.
Instead, we sat on the porch
and I ate what he peeled
and cleaned for me.
The scattering of the delicate
marine-colored shells across his lap
was something like what the ocean gives
the beach after a rain.

Father and Daughter

You are holding my sister in your arms.
She is but a few months old.
It is your day off,
beginning the night before
when you crawled out from under
the hull of an airplane
and wiping the grease from your hands,
said good-night to the two black boys
holding the kerosene lamp,
the only light for miles around.

In the colorless photograph,
thirty years later,
I can almost imagine that sun
as you pose in the backyard:
the hot white light of Coral Gables
momentarily blinding the two of you
in a halo of light. The white
edges of your cotton undershirt
hazy as if on fire. My sister
in her baby dress, starched and sweet-smelling.

I would be born four years
later, an unexpected birthday gift.
My arrival snuffing out her pink candles.
But until then,
it would be the two of you
together with my mother waving
occasionally through. At the screen door,
her heart-shaped face smiling distractedly
as she wipes her hands on a kitchen towel.

The small child you carried
in your arms filled your breathing
with the clover in the world:
a clean and fragrant handkerchief
folded to your breast,
worth more than money in your pocket.
And the next day you could slide
back under the whale-shaped,
metal belly of the plane,
a flashlight propped in your mouth
like a Havana cigar,
because you had been given something:
a daughter to sing to you,
a small voice
emerging from the unlit room at dusk.

A Mehinaku Girl in Seclusion

When the pequi fruit blossomed,
I went into seclusion.
A red flower
dropped out of my body
and stained the red dirt of the earth
one color. With one color
I became married to the earth.
I went to live by myself
in the hut at the end of the village.

There no one must see me.
For three years,
no one must touch me.
The men carve the spirit birds
and dream of me
becoming beautiful in the dark.
They say my skin
will be as delicate as the light
that touches the spider's web.
The women walk to the river
and bathe and time passes.

One woman, the old one,
brings me news of the harvest,
the names of the children who are born.
The children are taught
to make babies out of mud,
babies in the shape of gourds.
The children cry when the rains come.

When the rain comes I slip out
and circle the dirt plaza.
I pause as if to drink at each door.
At each door,
the sound of the sleeping.
I return before the first
hint of light,
return to hear
the click of my spinning.

I will learn to become
mistress of the hammocks.
The man who will be my husband
shall be proud.
When I walk beside him
to bathe in the river,
I will say with my body,
He is mine.
The manioc bread he eats
becomes the children I will bear.
His hammocks are not tattered.
Ask him. Yes, ask him.
I am learning to say this
with my body.

The Wind in the Trees

clears the morning of doves.
You remember the loneliness,
the loneliness you knew as a child
when everyone in the house was busy.
The house would smell of frying then

and your parents would move
back and forth across the room,
their shadows overlapping like swords.
And when they were free,

remember the sunlight
on your hands,
the light and dark side of a fist.
The wind pulling on your face like water.
In a carriage you traveled anciently,

a blanket tucked around your lap.
No one asked you anything.
No one pointed out the trees.
Then as an afterthought

you were remembered and
a cracker was crumbled onto your tray.
Little Bird they called you, *Little Bird*.
You could expect a frivolous squeeze.
Perhaps a feather under the chin.

There wasn't much you wouldn't do.
Lost in the folds
of the voluminous drapes one morning
you heard someone say,
look how cleverly the child plays.

And your mother clapped pleasantly
as you scuttled back and forth,
like a beetle or a mouse,
terrified and trapped,
repeating the act.

Today you remember the loneliness
in the small figure of your son
scooting by like a clown
on a red and yellow tricycle.
His intrepid feet,
posing as pedals,

kicking up the dust of the carpet.
Say goodbye and he waves
at the children going to school.
Their lunch pails and rain jackets

are the bright objects
bobbing below the window box.
Say anything. Say love
and he will lean to press

his cheek against the floor.

Arthur Sze

Ramona Sakiestewa

Born in 1950, **Arthur Sze** received his B.A. from the University of California at Berkeley in 1972, graduating Phi Beta Kappa. He is the author of four books: *The Willow Wind* (Rainbow Zenith Press, 1972; revised edition, Tooth of Time Books, 1981); *Two Ravens* (Tooth of Time Books, 1976; revised edition, 1984); *Dazzled* (Floating Island Publications, 1982); and *River River* (Lost Roads Publishers, 1987). His numerous awards include National Endowment for the Arts Writer-in-Residence Grants (1979, 1980, 1982), Witter Bynner Foundation for Poetry Grants (1980, 1982, 1989), a Creative Writing Fellowship from the National Endowment for the Arts (1982), and a fellowship from the George A. and Eliza Gardner Howard Foundation (1991). Currently, he is Director of the Creative Writing Program at the Institute of American Indian Arts in Santa Fe, New Mexico.

The Network

In 1861, George Hew sailed in a rowboat
from the Pearl river, China, across
the Pacific ocean to San Francisco.
He sailed alone. The photograph of him
in a museum disappeared. But, in the mind,
he is intense, vivid, alive. What is
this fact but another fact in a world
of facts, another truth in a vast network
of truths? It is a red maple leaf
flaming out at the end of its life,
revealing an incredibly rich and complex
network of branching veins. We live
in such a network: the world is opaque,
translucent, or, suddenly, lucid,
vibrant. The air is alive and hums
then. Speech is too slow to the mind.
And the mind's speech is so quick it breaks
the sound barrier and shatters glass.

The Leaves of a Dream Are
the Leaves of an Onion

1

Red oak leaves rustle in the wind.
Inside a dream, you dream the leaves
scattered on dirt, and feel it
as an instance of the chance configuration

to your life. All night you feel
red horses galloping in your blood,
hear a piercing siren, and are in love
with the inexplicable. You walk

to your car, find the hazard lights
blinking: find a rust-brown knife, a trout,
a smashed violin in your hands.
And then you wake, inside the dream,

to find tangerines ripening in the silence.
You peel the leaves of the dream
as you would peel the leaves off an onion.
The layers of the dream have no core,

no essence. You find a tattoo of
a red scorpion on your body.
You simply laugh, shiver in the frost,
and step back into the world.

2

A Galapagos turtle has nothing to do
with the world of the neutrino.
The ecology of the Galapagos Islands
has nothing to do with a pair of scissors.
The cactus by the window has nothing to do
with the invention of the wheel.
The invention of the telescope
has nothing to do with a red jaguar.
No. The invention of the scissors
has everything to do with the invention of the telescope.
A map of the world has everything to do
with the cactus by the window.
The world of the quark has everything to do
with a jaguar circling in the night.
The man who sacrifices himself and throws a Molotov
cocktail at a tank has everything to do
with a sunflower that bends to the light.

3

Open a window and touch the sun,
or feel the wet maple leaves flicker in the rain.
Watch a blue crab scuttle in clear water,
or find a starfish in the dirt.
Describe the color green to the color blind,
or build a house out of pain.

The world is more than you surmise.
Take the pines, green-black, slashed by light,
etched by wind, on the island
across the riptide body of water.
Describe the thousand iridescent needles
to a blind albino Tarahumara.

In a bubble chamber, in a magnetic field,
an electron spirals and spirals in to the center,
but the world is more than such a dance:
a spiraling in to the point of origin,
a spiraling out in the form of a
wet leaf, a blue crab, or a green house.

4

The heat ripples ripple the cactus.
Crushed green glass in a parking lot
or a pile of rhinoceros bones
give off heat, though you might not notice it.

The heat of a star can be measured
under a spectrometer, but not
the heat of the mind, or the heat of Angkor Wat.
And the rubble of Angkor Wat

gives off heat; so do apricot blossoms
in the night, green fish, black bamboo,
or a fisherman fishing in the snow.
And an angstrom of shift turns the pleasure

into pain. The ice that rips the fingerprint
off your hand gives off heat;
and so does each moment of existence.
A red red leaf, disintegrating in the dirt,

burns with the heat of an acetylene flame.
And the heat rippling off
the tin roof of the adobe house
is simply the heat you see.

5

What is the secret to a Guarneri violin?
Wool dipped in an indigo bath turns bluer
when it oxidizes in the air. Marat is
changed in the minds of the living.
A shot of tequila is related to Antarctica
shrinking. A crow in a bar or red snapper on ice
is related to the twelve tone method
of composition. And what does the tuning of tympani
have to do with the smell of your hair?
To feel, at thirty, you have come this far—
to see a bell over a door as a bell
over a door, to feel the care and precision
of this violin is no mistake, nor is the
sincerity and shudder of passion by which you live.

6

Crush an apple, crush a possibility.
No single method can describe the world;
therein is the pleasure
of chaos, of leaps in the mind.
A man slumped over a desk in an attorney's office
is a parrot fish caught in a seaweed mass.
A man who turns to the conversation in a bar
is a bluefish hooked on a cigarette.
Is the desire and collapse of desire in an unemployed carpenter
the instinct of salmon to leap upstream?
The smell of eucalyptus can be incorporated
into a theory of aggression.
The pattern of interference in a hologram
replicates the apple, knife, horsetails on the table,
but misses the sense of chaos, distorts
in its singular view. Then
touch, shine, dance, sing, be, becoming, be.

Every Where and Every When

1

Catch a moth in the Amazon; pin it under glass.
See the green-swirling magenta-flecked wings

miming a fierce face. And dead, watch it fly.
Throw a piece of juniper into a fire.

Search out the Odeon in Zurich to find Lenin or Klee.
No one has a doctrine of recollection to

bring back knowledge of what was, is?
The Odeon cafe is not the place to look

for Lenin's fingerprint. The piece of burning juniper
has the sound of the bones of your hands

breaking. And the moth at the window, magenta-flecked,
green-swirling, is every where and every when.

2

Everything is supposed to fit: mortise and tenon,
arteries and veins, hammer, anvil, stirrup in the ear,

but it does not fit. Someone was executed
today. Tomorrow friends of the executed will execute

the executers. And this despair is the intensifying
fever and chill, in shortening intervals,

of a malaria patient. Evil is not a variety of
potato found in the Andes. The smell of a gardenia

is not scissors and sponge in the hands of
an inept surgeon. Everything is supposed to fit:

but wander through Cuzco and the orientation of
streets and plazas is too Spanish. Throw

hibiscus on a corpse. Take an aerial view;
see the city built in the shape of a jaguar's head.

3

I pick a few mushrooms in the hills,
but do not know the lethal from the edible.

I cannot distinguish red wool dyed
with cochineal or lac, but know that

cochineal with alum, tin, salt and lime juice
makes a rosé, a red, a burgundy.

Is it true an anti-matter particle
never travels as slow as the speed of light,

and, colliding with matter, explodes?
The mind shifts as the world shifts.

I look out the window, watch Antares glow.
The world shifts as the mind shifts;

or this belief, at least, increases
the pleasure of it all—the smell of espresso

in the street, picking blueberries,
white-glazed, blue-black,

sieved gold from a river, this moment
when we spin and shine.

Black Java Pepper

Despair, anger, grief:
as a seiner indiscriminately hauls
humpies, jellyfish, kelp,
we must—farouche,

recalcitrant—conversely
angle for sockeye.
Our civilization has no genetic code
to make wasps return

each spring to build a nest
by the water heater
in the shed. We must—igneous,
metamorphic—despite

such plans as to push Mt. Fuji into the ocean
to provide more land—
grind cracked black
Java pepper into our speech

so that—limestone into marble,
granite into gneiss—
we become through our griefs—
rain forest islands—song.

Jeff Tagami

Marc Ancheta

Jeff Tagami was born in 1954 in Watsonville, California. His book *October Light* was published by Kearny Street Workshop Press in 1987. He cotranslated *This Wanting to Sing: Asian Poets in South America* (Contact II Press) and coedited *Without Names* (Kearny Street Workshop Press), a Bay Area Filipino American poetry anthology. After fourteen years in San Francisco, he recently returned to Watsonville, where he lives with his wife and two sons.

Song of Pajaro

Pajaro the men thigh deep in mud
who are cutting cauliflower
the tractor they must depend
to pull them out
the catering truck selling hot coffee

Pajaro the children who clean
the mud from their father's boots
They sleep   They wake
to the smell of cauliflower growing
in fields that are not dreams
fields that begin under their bedroom windows
and end in a world they do not know
from the mountains to the river
from the river to the beach

Now Pajaro is tired   It wants to sleep
The packing sheds shut down for the night
The trucks close their trailer doors
and the Southern Pacific leaves town
(having got what it wanted)

This Pajaro of my mother leaving work
who at this moment is crossing the bridge of no lights
in her Buick Electra with wings like a huge bird
crossing over the black river toward home
where she will make the sign of the cross
over the cooked rice in the name of the Lord
and prepare for the table
a steaming plate of cauliflower.

Tobera

My name is Fermin.
I am twenty-two,
forever.
I work all day.
I tip a bottle of bourbon
and swallow four times.
I'm as strong as hell.

It wasn't always this way . . .

Before,
I was serenaded
by a band that played
a slow waltz
and around me danced
five pale-skinned women
whose eyes were blackened
by make-up. My head swooned
from the scent of perfume
and my body grew weak
until the music stopped
and I remembered
there was a room full
of other men waiting
in line for a chance
to dance with these women
and I was at the end
of this line.

Such was the power of my desire.

So I carried my desire
to work with me.
I carried it over my shoulder
like my hoe.
It was in my hoe.
When I swung it,
desire cut the weeds
between the long rows
of sugar beet
and my desire sweetened
throughout the day
until it grew dark
and my eyes,
which were separate
from my desire,
could no longer see
and it was time to return
to the bunkhouse
and drink and drink
until my desire blurred
along with my seeing
and I fell asleep.

Desire, not loneliness
bought the tickets
to hang around my neck
like a braided rope
until we were a flock
of men unashamed
to spend a week's wage
for a dance.
Yes, a man gets lonely,
but he has to do something
to stop from going crazy.
And it's not craziness
when men get together
to buy a '29 Model T
and drive from Watsonville
to Lompoc, San Pedro

to Oxnard and back again
past the neatly clipped lawns
of white neighborhoods
where they are not wanted
in a country
where they are not welcome.
And to do this over and over
like a man slapping
his own face again and again.

I am not bitter, believe me.
I've got a place
I call home
where I can lay my head
on a clean pillow sheet.
There are men
I can call *brother*.
Here is my shed.
Here are all
my tools, my garden.
If it pleases me,
I can walk to the river
and stand under the bridge
while, above me, white
families rush back
and forth in their cars.
I can feel their laughter
against my back
in the railing's vibration.

I could be happy.

This is how I return
to my bed each night
with a smile on my face
because I know what awaits me,
Listen.
Here comes the buzzing
of the bullet

which bears my name.
It's a bee looking
for the hive of my neck
and I must lay still
for its sweet entrance.
Time moves on.
My brothers grow older
without me and I
become the cold breath
on their necks, the blind
Fog in the field.
I am not spiteful,
just a reminder
when things are going well.

This is all my desire demands, now.

Remember me?
I'm Fermin, the young one,
forever twenty-two
whose name is forming
like a dead son, even now,
on the pursed lips
of my brothers whispering,
"Tobera, Tobera, Tobera."

As a result of the Watsonville race riots of 1930 and tension brought on by a Palm Beach taxi dance, Fermin Tobera, a Filipino laborer, was shot and killed by three local high school youths as he lay sleeping in his bunk at a labor camp in Murphy's Crossing. The youths were never convicted of the killing. Tobera's body was returned to the Philippines where a National Day of Humiliation was held.

Mussel Rock/Lowtide—
Santa Cruz, California 1959

Fog lifting above the fields
and camphouses of many windows.
In a small cove, the families of Filipinos
gather mussels, stooping over rocks
that rise up, dripping, from the low waters.
The girl, who suffers from elephantiasis,
collects starfish, pushing her enormous legs
from rock to rock. The boy, who grows old
before our eyes, pokes a stick at the washed-up
jellyfish. He is a tiny, wrinkled man
dressed in the clothes of a child. He moves on
to stab the heart of the opening sea anemone.
All the old-time bachelors, off from work,
join the married men on the rocks and loosen,
with crowbars, the clinging mussel shells,
stacking them into burlap sacks.
They are called names that sound like
Cook Song, Sip Pee, Cowl Bo, Long Hand, Bar Tick.

Laughter and the clanging of pots
on the beach, the American wives
start up the fires with driftwood and steam
the mussels open. They are happy
in their one-piece bathing suits and hair-dos,
their hard liquor and gossip. When one bends
over the pot, there is a loud popping, and cinders
fly out from the fire. Then come the squeals
of the other women, pointing to the puckered cup
of her bathing suit where her falsie had slipped
out into the flames.

After everyone crowds around the steaming pots
to eat, somebody's wife makes a joke
about the mussel's orange vulva lips and black
pubic cilia. The giggle spreads among the women,
the husbands slurping soup, the timid bachelor
who blushes and the children asking, "What, what?"
Mounds of discarded shells, grandmothers go back
to sunning themselves, peeling their thick nylons
down ankles, children drag branches of balloon-like
seaweed through the sand, fathers and mothers drowse,
arms wrapped around each other.

       Sun low on the horizon,
the last door slams shut, packing in all the tired,
the girl clutching starfish to her breast and smelling
of the ocean, the boy, dying of old age, who points
to the rocks slowly submerging as the waves of his own
hair slowly whiten. Along the bumpy road, the cars
stir dust that rises and settles on the young heads
of brussel sprouts, on the single men walking home
to their bunkhouse and its windows
burning, now, a brilliant orange.

Delaina Thomas

Franco Salmoiraghi

Delaina Thomas was born in 1955 and raised in Hawaii. Half-Okinawan, she received her B.A. from the University of Hawaii and her M.F.A. from the University of California at Irvine. Her poems have appeared in *Bamboo Ridge Quarterly*, *Hawaii Review*, *Hudson Review*, *Ironwood*, and *Missouri Review*. She works part-time in the Poets-in-the-School Program and as a teacher of the Transcendental Meditation Program.

The Turning of the Year

I do not live in the depthless cool
wherein black marigolds glimmer on the pond
and irises let through light like prisms

without colorations or subjectivity

I do not like the jadeflower claw at wind
or sky as the crayfish who reposes to green summarily

summarily I live
taking the surfaces of things as causes
whereas it is in the depths and depthless that purposes begin
where flower names hang like banners in space
and wolves' teeth are strung like chimes
as were mine by the skeleton dentist in childhood dreams

the garden spider sits restive
not sure of its fate
though it is black it sees beauty in its legs
stretched out radial like any star's to the human eye
and wonders why the newlywed jumps and shrieks
at the sight of it on silk
elegant webwork
it wants to wail at her unlike perception
as she slaps it with the *zori*

the grey fur of the cat ruffles
in the wind hair by hair
on the road
no one picks it up because someone else will
the fur gets flatter with each passing tire
blood scars widen on the haunches

in the huts of selves
smudged and meager the hands stretch
over the eyes ignorant

I wonder at the beauty
of these fragments
not a joke or sadism keeps them vibrant
their existence real at each particular level
but farther into the depthless I wander
where silence clings like juice
of the crownflower to the shoulders
lingers like fragrance of old *maile* in the memory
sends a wince of pleasure like *lilikoi* through the tastebuds

fruits of labor fruits of pleasure
the life turning over the year
like a sage *koi* its belly to moonlight

where have I been swimming and where am I to go

because of the tirednesses
like skins that grow grey through time over the senses
till the soul looks like a praying mantis nest
in a vacuum
forgotten by the kindergartener at recess
in a *daikon* jar without holes for circulation

the soul that was the blue flame of the flame
only the wick of the candle left
grey like *hinahina*
hanging from the mangotree
and crumble pieces blow off
in the breezes to grace the grass
of the swollen grave of the *imu*

until some tribe comes travelling
of clouds

the young mother in tall green heels
rushes to get out sliding the closet door closed
her child's hand jammed
there are no accidents only carelessness
what was she thinking of that made her mind lapse
dancing by trees lit with snow or bells

the swirl everyone wants to remember

the dance of particles in a rainbow
or dust in a sunray beaming to the floor
iridescents on buds of blueginger
sparkle off into the moonlight
flowercrackers

she won't hear them
my grandmother who won't speak
sitting waiting for death week after month
shrunken except for the abdomen where nine fetuses grew
sunmoles enlarged gums worn thin
refusing to eat more favorites all the time
shrimp *tempura* then *sushi* to even *okai*
"*shiru*" she wants to drink only "*shiru*"

she won't chop back the shellginger
or plant stalks of green onion
will not look in the mirror two years
or at the infant greatgrandchild

I looked wandering in the depthless

the scorpion dipped in honey
who approached me
his intensity was appealing
I got so into his inner city sculptures
he could not let me leave Guanajuato finally
as he wrapped his hands around my neck
I thought how refined his fingers were

nonetheless I could not breathe
and so pressed my palm against the pane
until it fell to the courtyard below
in the shatter he lost his grip
I ran out
but years later as I settled into the depthless
yellowing gardenia scent in through the louvers
I saw the drawn bones of her that he shaped of me
in the twilight swimming around the trunks
of the pepper trees
the arms much longer than these
as though reaching farther was needed
but the hands drooped to the knees futilely.

remembering death
with new eyes
looking at my son
my own prospect seldom shook me
but to think of his

to drifting off like a machine on automatic
washing pots and flatware
caring how dust webs and strands line hinges of doorways
attacking the invaders of time and fading
that age upholstery
by smoking the windows
she never could get enough light out of the house my mother
claimed she swam too many summers at Palama pool in the glare
my grandmother following in sunglasses to her chair
by the television images and radiation
steadily deadening the hours

alongside in the garden
the *skink* flits in and out of *lau'ae*
my son gesticulates at sky
or crotons gold and glassgreen
spots to burgundy

as I step out into the depthless

black pondwaters lapping at my ankles
I wade deeper into the quagmire of flowers
because I hold not enough
dearness for desolation
to turn back

to where adventitious banyan roots drape down
and beyond the moth flapping shadows
there Uncle Chock plays the *ukulele*
fleas jumping across the strings
who lived on easy with a bottle of whiskey
was raised *hanai* and claimed to be Andy Cummings' half brother
gambled in Chinatown and played pool with the gang
all day the day Massie made her claim
who always had a freezer full of fish
from friends at the wharf
and got Prince Hanalei his fist gig
as Gabby his at Chocksee By the Sea
one morning he smashed his Martin to bits
then went walking
and was found two weeks later
at Fort Shafter in a drainage ditch
the three carat diamond gone from his finger
Sharon murmured reverently "Daddy always said
da old Chinese walk toward da mountains
when dey die"
legends are men I have known
and beside him the Portuguese neighbor Catholic devout
four cattleyas nestled in her frenchtwist
who swooned in front of me
at his funeral of three hundred admirers
and was carried off her sympathy too close
the plaster Madonna
graces her lawn still
lit with Christmas lights
along Notley Lane

cumulus with vertical growth
bringing afternoon showers
to the valley

and something leaps up from the wicks
desire or will
to breathe again and see

even the garbage miracle
oilpools in the garage floor
mixing with rain trailing to the gutter
rainbowflowers
and my outdated clothes spill from the tidy drawers
to volunteer for the Salvation Army
and once and for all old loves are swept away
by tides of the stiff broom without further examination
and the unanswered mail answers itself

deeper released in the depths

the heaviness in my body
surface to my awareness
matted in the shoulders
terracing the brow they press to get out
I focus inward on the energies how they flow
tensing vocal chords and halt
needled in the soles of the feet
I surrender to timeless rest sinking deeper without effort
against the wills and fears of shadows
who plea for the life of their own
red coral branches in the whites of my eyes diminish
as I steep in bluewater
the dull ache in my solar plexus clears
loosening gradually the networks of radii and meridians
spanning the nervous system
unwinding stresses like impressions from lifetimes
of little agonies that take their toll

and bigger ones looming
that lift smoking
as they dissipate

slowly from the process I wake to sunlight riding currents of water evenly

fine jewels climb back onto my person
my soul starts to feel true again
and it is not a strange reflection in the glass
the face unlined
eyes directly friendly
pearls at her wrist
the smile echoes back into my image
her tone in my ears a wavering
like riverwater over stones and reeds green
long river quietly
river
until no sound
makes wind on the lips
and no sensation remains
so water glides over the body
without reminding it of its boundaries
wet crystal on the clavicle
dew-wets on the lids cool

mist rising blue on the slopes of memory

for I can't resist looking back
as I tie the *kadomatsu* to the porchposts
and the last hours of the year approach
only a few stubborn Chinese
like Mr. Young next door have bothered
to get a religious license for firecrackers
illegal this year for the first time
he'll burn them toward midnight near the slopes of Manoa graveyard
to symbolize the process
or concretely impel it
of casting demons out from the body
or the house

I go in to line the altar with fern
and lacquer vases of anthurium and bird-of-paradise
gilded lotuses rest at the feet of Buddha
I brush flour from the *mochi* cakes
and stack them two by two
topping each with a tangerine
Auntie Ethel unrolls the scrolls of old Japanese men with huge earlobes
one a fisherman holds a red snapper over his head
another wields a *taiko* in one hand
and a sack of rice over the other shoulder
chrysanthemums blue on his robe drift like clouds
toward the one next to him
whose bald head is vertically elongated
he passes beads of a rosary through his fingers
though the brows of the man in the center are menacing
he too manages a smile in his coat of mail
holding a miniature temple in one hand
and a spear in the other
his banners red tasseled undulate in the wind
as his thin goatee lifts slightly
the fattest one of them is unshaven
his chest exposed is hairy also
playing a purple *shamisen*
his smile looks the most benevolent of all
high above the assembly
a stork flies past the red sun

I fill the jiggers with whiskey
for Ojichan and Uncle Daji
and light the candles and *senko*
I don't know a prayer in Japanese
so I stand a moment hands clasped
and try to think something meaningful
or just of the individual dead resting hopefully
then leave so my grandmother can inspect
the one preparation she still cares to

I go to the kitchen to join cousins
cutting rolles of *sushi*
and pouring *mochi* soup
and because I love the watery crunch
of the sclerenchyma
surrounding its xylem tubes
I eat fresh lotus root
for longevity
of life

outside the aerials in the night sky
cometing green and sapphire
for a moment one forgets everything
but the beauty
celestial display manmade
Constellations sizzle violet
as I count the minutes to midnight
they rise one after another
swaying like kites when wind sags
or like the head of the liondog in the *bon* dance
flowering into Starbursts
trailing smoketails across the roof
the Colored Pearls roll up cerise and gold
and Roman Candles track astral paths through the eucalyptus trees
neighbors on the sidewalk shake hands and cheer
gladness being alive for the turning of the year

Amy Uyematsu

Amy Uyematsu, a third-generation Japanese American, lives in Los Angeles with her son. She is a member of PAAWWW (Pacific Asian American Women Writers West) and coedited *ROOTS: An Asian American Reader* (UCLA, 1970). Her poems have been published in journals and anthologies such as *Poetry/LA, Bamboo Ridge,* and *Amerasia Journal.* Her first book, *30 Miles from J-Town* (Story Line Press, 1992), is the 1992 Nicholas Roerich Contest winner.

Near Roscoe and Coldwater

(the Northeast San Fernando Valley, 1985)

i. Sunday

This is a busy corner.
Truckdrivers, businessmen, lowriders,
all slow down to view
the building of the Thai temple.
On the vacant lot next to gas stations
and a closed down 7-11, the roof of gold appears.
Barefoot men in orange robes
plant grass and small shade trees.
Every Sunday immigrants drive in,
they follow the light
reflected in the golden roof.
I hear chanting sounds and afterwards
the easy laughter of families
cooking lunch on outdoor grills.
They fill the neighborhood with Eastern scents,
above the car fumes and dry weed.

ii. Boy's Story

He is eighteen and no matter
how many times I mispronounce his name,
he always smiles, an old man's face.
I am his only Asian teacher
since he left Kampuchea.
I've read, argued, marched,
and now after seeing a film about the war,
I have the audacity to ask what he knows.
"My father killed by Khmer Rouge.
Brother killed too. Mother escaped,"

but he may never find her.
Still smiling, he tells me about
his new car. Now and then I see him,
cruising Victory Boulevard.

iii. The Crossing

Morning traffic has stopped.
A line of honking cars,
capable of crushing the small woman.
She is stuck at the railroad crossing,
the shopping cart of used cans and rags
too heavy for her thin body.
She looks like the Vietnamese grandmothers
I've seen so often in photographs,
especially her eyes
which tend
caravans of old men and babies.
Tireless eyes keeping vigil
in the seconds of animal silence, before
each approaching assault.
Drivers yell as she talks to herself
in her own language, but everyone watches
eyes that can sift
through earth, bone, metal, blood,
knowing which fragments to save.

The Same Month They Bombed Cambodia

—for Mary and John Kao

We open the street door,
three floors up over a noodle factory,
to a perfume thickened by frying things,
sweet sauces, freshly cut ducks and hens,
hot oil smells collide with leaking sewage pipes,
the stink from ten day garbage that won't be collected.
And the perfume still thickens—
the sesame scent of noodles
fills these narrow streets and air pockets
left between too many bodies,
sidewalks breathing oldness, poverty, sweat,
and new immigrant hustle.

A homemade poster—come to a health fair—
free pap smear . . . t.b. tests . . . child care provided.
This is how it could be, buy our newspaper and find out.

A cha shiu bao, the biggest I've ever eaten.

A Lower Eastside cockroach, the biggest I've seen—
lights switched on, my foot threatens, it refuses to run,
I learn to go to the bathroom with eyes closed.

A late night drinkoff—while we argue RCP, IWK, ASG,
and other wellknown initials, Charlie sings genocide.
China has millions, Japan its Sonies and Datsuns,
we'll be the scapegoat again, or we could move,
start new like our grandparents.

A book from Soho fashioned by Ting,
his penis on every third page—red, blue, pink, green.

A recipe for black beans on rice, copied from
the Cuban who goes by the name Jorge Chan.

An afternoon watching painters on flying ladders
free the entire face of the ghetto skyscraper—
their favorite subjects the old women,
also peasant mothers wearing sandals and rifles.

A melody of kid chatter, white hair gossip,
each dialect smoothly inflected. Flirting talk,
bickering talk, cursing crying laughing talk,
some even think we belong,
look hard when we can't answer.

A bargain platter of spicy beef with peppers,
only $2.95—no charge for dinner show—
waiters jump white man who won't stop yelling chinks.

A walk towards Times Square with our Asian contingent,
no one warns us about the horses—we scatter,
the man with moustache and nightstick picks me.
I have long black hair like the Cambodians.

Nellie Wong

Haruko

Born in 1934, **Nellie Wong** received her B.A. from San Francisco State University. She has published two books, *Dreams in Harrison Railroad Park* (Kelsey Street Press, 1977) and *The Death of Long Steam Lady* (West End Press, 1986). In 1981, she was featured in Allie Light's documentary film, "Mitsuye & Nellie, Asian American Poets." Her work has appeared in numerous anthologies such as *This Bridge Called My Back: Writings by Radical Women of Color; Breaking Silence;* and *13th Moon: A Chinese American Poetry Anthology,* among others. In June 1983, she was a delegate to the First American Women Writers' Tour to China hosted by the Chinese Writers Association. Currently, she works as an Affirmative Action Analyst at the University of California, San Francisco.

Dreams in Harrison Railroad Park

We sit on a green bench in Harrison Railroad Park.
As we rest, I notice my mother's thighs
thin as my wrists.
I want to hug her
but I am afraid.

A bearded man comes by, asks for a cigarette.
We shake our heads, hold out our empty hands.
He shuffles away and picks up
a half-smoked stub.
His eyes light up.
Enclosed by the sun he dreams
temporarily.

Across the street an old woman hobbles by.
My mother tells me: She is unhappy here.
She thinks she would be happier
back home.
But she has forgotten.

My mother's neighbor dreams
of warm nights in Shanghai,
of goldfish swimming in a courtyard pond,
of having a young maid
anoint her tiny bound feet.

And my mother dreams
of wearing dresses that hang in her closet,
of swallowing soup without pain,
of coloring eggs
for an unborn grandson.

I turn and touch my mother's eyes.
They are wet
and I dream
and I dream
of embroidering
new skin.

Can't Tell

When World War II was declared
on the morning radio,
we glued our ears, widened our eyes.
Our bodies shivered.

A voice said
Japan was the enemy,
Pearl Harbor a shambles
and in our grocery store
in Berkeley, we were suspended

next to the meat market
where voices hummed,
valises, pots and pans packed,
no more hot dogs, baloney,
pork kidneys.

We children huddled on wooden planks
and my parents whispered:
We are Chinese, we are Chinese.
Safety pins anchored,
our loins ached.

Shortly our Japanese neighbors vanished
and my parents continued to whisper:
We are Chinese, we are Chinese.

We wore black arm bands,
put up a sign
in bold letters.

On Thinking of Photographing
My Fantasies

No, please don't,
don't photograph me
in my fantasies,
in my orange kimono
with blue and yellow chrysanthemums,
you might see
my legs
with roadmaps
leading
nowhere but down
to the toes
then up to my navel
where little hairs hide
and rise
to my breasts
spaces apart
to my arms
to my eyes
red from smog
my hair black yet greying.
Oh, yes, my fantasies,
lounging in a wicker chair,
posing nude, perhaps,
a cigarette dangling
from my lips
as I sit beneath palm leaves
beaded glass curtains
the wind swishing
mosquitos and gnats
onto my body
itching my fingers

wanting cool wine
wiping ants
off tiled drainboards
out into the garden
where the moon hides
between limbs
of the peony tree
into the courtyard
where mothers of my mother
might have scaled,
shuffling in tiny bound feet
to be sold
to feed
their families,
where the peasants and farmers
raise water buffalo, plant rice,
their backs stooped
to the sun and only after dark
nibble watermelon seeds
and the fathers of my father
separated from the mothers of my mother
gambling, drinking in cities perhaps
after toiling
in sundrenched fields
eating smiles of peach-skinned women
who fan them with feathers
marriages endured
for the paper names of families
across the miles
for crates of canned milk
and apricot nectar
and the music of lutes
of harps and mandolins
scarcely heard
in the ears of peasants
but in dreams and visions
of imperial life
beyond compounds

of water cranked from wells
of cooking rice
to wash the feet
and faces of husbands' parents
who take in daughters-in-law
for muscles
moving daybreak to dusk
where ghosts lurk
in beds of straw mattings
in the orchid bodies of women
who know no poems
but their own lives·
for keeping their eyes
leveled at the ground
grateful for not being drowned
or sold
in the shells
of watergourds
allowing the past
the mythologies
to stream forth
like milk from mothers' breasts
into bamboo hollows
time machines flying
like golden phoenixes
telling story after story
to ears untrained for the onslaught
of droughts, monsoons, thunder
where villagers eat pork
if the meat-man comes by,
dirt roads
leading out
to green, the underside
of oceans and skies
where skin and bones
collide with stars
what eyes refuse
to see, what mouths refuse

to talk, tongues cut in infancy
for golden retreats
for the intimacy
of people who think
they know you
because you know
not yet your selves
for lacquer, for brass,
for snow-flower plums
salivating your mouth
and the fuzzy squash
of days and nights
fisted in gnarled hands
and legs just learning
to walk
on levees
on lakes
and rainwashed forests
for the light
of small clearings
where your heart
hones your mind,
the silver bolt
you now hold
in your moving hands

On Plaza Garibaldi

The mariachi beckon, their guitars,
their violins string themselves,
me, striated
among the people.

Their smiles, their eyes plead for work.
No barrier this language.
I am their teeth.

Meandering I watch the fountain
gush promises in this twilight,
this scene. This is truly Mexican,
someone told me.

Barbecued goat's meat, ears of corn,
platters of flan assault my eyes.
I am afraid. My stomach has a mean streak.
I apologize for it.

A little girl tugs at my sleeve,
"peso, por favor?"
I want to gather her, smell flowers
but her mother is watching.

At the edge of the plaza
a young girl leans against a gray wall.
She is a donut, half raised.
The men who watch her
finger themselves
inside their pockets.

I tell myself:
I am not she, I am not she.
She is someone else's
sister.

Picnic

Each Sunday I climb the mountain to picnic
with my mother and father in their twin coats,
breathing air
that only the mountains can give,
air as fresh as carp swimming upstream.

These Sundays my mother and father and I talk.
Oh, how we talk and talk!
Of apples and lace and cloth bound books,
of sour plums that make our mouths water,
changing expressions on our putty faces.

Although we talk together, we three,
we promise each other nothing. Not trees,
not oranges, not fish
for it is not our time to be fenced in,
not when spring promises its own
flowering quince.

I hold my mother's and father's hands tightly,
drinking the pools of their eyes.
It is strange we communicate now,
this way,
where there are no phones.

Together we celebrate the Tiger's Year.
We feast on chicken, mushrooms and the monk's dish,
pregnant with its cellophane noodles and fine black hair.
Our laughter is perfumed with incense
that the spirits drink.

We swim, drunk with the sea in our ears,
as seagulls swoop down to eat with us.
They are welcome guests and sit on my father's knees
which are still knobby and my mother is still
telling him what to do.

Look! The swallows are building their nests
and we toast what little ricewine is left.
The chrysanthemums bend their heads.
I gather fresh lichee and leave my mother and father
my only silk coverlet.

Kathleen McClung

David Woo was born in Phoenix, Arizona, in 1959. He studied English at Stanford and Harvard, and Chinese at Yale. For four years, he taught English at universities in China, including one year as the Beijing coordinator of Volunteers in Asia, an American nonprofit organization. He was a 1990–92 Wallace Stegner fellow in poetry at Stanford, and his poems have appeared in *The New Yorker* and *ZYZZYVA*. He lives in San Francisco, where he is at work on his first book-length collection.

Eden

Yellow-oatmeal flowers of the windmill palms
like brains lashed to fans—
even they think of cool paradise,

not this sterile air-conditioned chill
or the Arizona hell in which they sway becomingly.
Every time I return to Phoenix I see these palms

as a child's height marks on a kitchen wall,
taller now than the yuccas they were planted with,
taller than the Texas sage trimmed

to a perfect gray-green globe with pointillist
lavender blooms, taller than I,
who stopped growing years ago and commenced instead

my slow, almost imperceptible slouch
to my parents' old age:
Father's painful bend—really a bending of a bend—

to pick up the paper at the end of the sidewalk;
Mother, just released from Good Samaritan,
curled sideways on a sofa watching the soaps,

an unwanted tear inching down
at the plight of some hapless Hilary or Tiffany.
How she'd rail against television as a waste of time!

Now, with one arthritis-mangled hand,
she aims the remote control at the set
and flicks it off in triumph, turning to me

as I turn to the trees framed in the Arcadia door.
Her smile of affection melts into the back of my head,
a throb that presses me forward,

hand pressed to glass. I feel the desert heat
and see the beautiful shudders of the palms in the yard
and wonder why I despised this place so,

why I moved from city to temperate city, anywhere
without palms and cactus trees.
I found no paradise, as my parents know,

but neither did they, with their eager sprinklers
and scrawny desert plants pumped up to artificial splendor,
and their lives sighing away, exhaling slowly,

the man and woman
who teach me now as they could not before
to prefer real hell to any imaginary paradise.

Grandfather's Rockery

The verge bore the remnants of his shearings,
green splinters on red gravel, where he knelt
to the earth to sight his plane of grass:
flat as he could make it. And the blooms—

pink-veined sorrels, star-petaled, yellow glaring
bracts—made a long, scraggly *S* alongside,
to "undo the symmetry," he said, marking for us
his own boundary between order and chaos.

Oh, he believed in repression: his shears
cutting the uneven cowlicks of grass,
shaping his flowers to the desired asymmetry—
even in chaos a delineation. And the jagged

lines of his rockery—Guilin's peaks reduced
to the crude essence of karst edges—struggled
to hold back, scale back, the imposing presence
of remembered mountains. Their majesty, too,

was miniaturized like a transistor or microchip,
so that we would peer into the stone hollows,
the tiny carp lake, and see nothing, splendors
too subtle to perceive. Only in his memory

were they ordered, real, hugely present.
It was a mercy, then, that his circuitry
should be clotted as with dust, and his eyes
blind to the spectacle of a body—his own—

sprawling across the prim gravel verge,
jutting over the carefully clipped lawn,
while we trampled the flowers to reach him
and the rockery cast its indifferent shadows.

Expatriates

We walked across a frozen river in Manchuria,
my traveling companions and I. Dogs howled
from the distant bank, and a train
rode backward on a cantilever bridge,
the plume of smoke leaning the other way,
eager as a child waving goodbye.

I said I couldn't think of two people I'd rather
shiver with, and both of them shivered
in agreement. Even with their dog-fur caps
and their People's Liberation Army overcoats
and their padded lime-green boots,
they ambled along with an American grace,
radiant as the ice that held beneath our feet.

When we reached Sun Island, we played
hide-and-go-seek among the barren poplars
and the old Russian dachas. I was first,
calling out the numbers and observing
with furtive glances the backs of my friends
as they glided behind boles and slipped
behind splintery cottages and tumbled over
the snow-heaped bank and onto the ice:
swirls of green and brown against a stark white
backdrop, my beautiful, temporary friends,
small and round and dizzy as the world
we had flown across.

The Great Helmsman

Why did the clerk drag his fingertips
    over the abacus and tell me, through yawn
        and smirk and drone, No, there aren't any,

no tomatoes, when I could see them heaped
    in red and green piles behind him? Oh,
        I took it personally at the time, stormed

out of the store—Foodstuffs Shop No. 6—
    rode fiercely through the streets of Beijing,
        poplar shadows flicking across my face,

and stopped, deadended, at a tiny station
    in a snatch of countryside—fallow sorghum
        and rice paddies, Gobi desert dust. I leaned

my bike against the flaking walls, their
    Mao slogans whitewashed but still visible—
        "Our Great Helmsman," "The reddest red sun

of our hearts rising in the East"—and sat
    and gulped the bitter smoke of a Great Wall
        cigarette. What horrid vengeance I conjured up:

the smirk widening in the earth like some
    unrecorded disaster from another dynasty,
        all the cretinous bureaucrats and sour-faced

clerks sucked in, easily, like that. And,
    as if to confirm that cruel heaven approved
        of such a fate, I looked up to see a poster

peeling in the corner, just below the characters
   for "helmsman": the photo was lovely and round,
      reds mixed with purples, an intricate blossom

like a chrysanthemum, and I sighed and thought,
   How pretty, until I saw the caption beneath,
      "No combustibles on the trains," and realized

it was the exploded remains of a human head.

Habit

The habit of staring
at a stranger's profile
in the teeming deli
or off-hour café,
the habit of looking away,
tilting your face into your *Times,*
grazing the squeaky white rim
of your espresso cup,
looking away from the face that looks back
with interest or disdain or suspicion,
in infinite gradations,
like the faces of those who shed
their strangeness and became your friends—
the face of Anna, who smiled serenely,
or Yang Ping, who furrowed his brow,
or Martin, who grimaced—
the habit of seeing in a stranger's
accidental gesture
or deliberate expression,
the finger patting the side of the jaw,
the pull, tiny, discreet,
of an earlobe or disheveled collar,
even the clumsy wink,
the leer, the rapacious grin,
the habit of seeing in any attitude
what Baudelaire called
the glance that brought him back to life,
played over and over again
in the faces of others,
reviving you, resuscitating you,
propelling you back into yourself
or, better yet, out of yourself—
how weary you are of yourself!
even in April,
in the melting city,
the passersby, the *flâneurs,*
acknowledging you exist,
their eyes turning to yours
and staring back,
bloodshot or clear,
it doesn't matter,
you've become their habit, too,
like an afternoon cup of *caffè latte;*
white foam you lick
from your upper lip
as a stranger smiles.

John Yau

John Yau was born in 1950, in Lynn, Massachusetts. He received his B.A. from Bard College and his M.F.A. from Brooklyn College. An art critic and curator, his reviews and essays frequently appear in *Artforum, Arts,* and *Art Space.* He has received a fellowship from the NEA (1977–78); two Ingram Merrill Fellowships (1979–80, 1985–86); a New York Foundation for the Arts Fellowship (1988); Lavan Award for Younger Poets from the Academy of American Poets (1988); and General Electric Foundation Award for Younger Writers (1988). In 1983, *Corpse and Mirror* was selected by John Ashbery to appear in the National Poetry Series. His *Radiant Silhouette: New and Selected Work 1974–1988* was published in 1989 by Black Sparrow Press, who will publish his *Edificio Sayonara* in 1992.

Radiant Silhouette I

Blue leather harness slips off glistening shoulders
A row of whispers burns on the windowsill

The company motto: Don't count
your scalps before they're dried

I am stapled to the listening post
scanning glass beads and loose teardrops

A lean stalk of sharkskin
on a high frequency appetite surge

I am gnawing the edge of my dusty tongue
when another profile jolts the screen

slips through the twilight crevices
Camera shadow trap evaluates commodity status

defines risk probability
I remember when spring was blue and green

and ants were crushed on the museum's steps
Now, someone's emerald shadow

glows beneath the slab of a dead volcano night
and archaic language splinters

float to the surface of the dream
Do you want to watch me dance

until I evaporate
The soup is ripe

with flies
The laugh pools

have eroded
but I still miss your bee stung lips

Talk to me, the voice whispers
Talk to me, and I'm halfway home

Radiant Silhouette II

There is no place in this dark
to huddle

no music that hears us
singing

All this stood up on the world
until incendiary units filed their reports

I am the pile stranded in front of the window
monitoring her blue aluminum eyes

Someone whispers
Old habits are hard

and thin
yet she still sleeps in her hair

A woman points to herself
as if she were a foreign language

I am one of many swathed in fire
a tangerine hanging on the south wall

Bring me my head on a shoe
Bring me the remnants that are mine

so I may tend to their festering
My smile is washable

I have hurled a spear of lightning
into the camera

I have dredged it up

Radiant Silhouette III

Baudelaire took the train
from Paris to Rome

a pink skull and blue pear
balanced on the tray beside him

My mother saw hideous diseases
whenever I spoke

something to be expunged from the filthy air
he whispered

pointing to his bird wing shadow
I had to learn to erase the mirror

when I reached for the pen
ignore the ink-stained butterfly

hovering above
a painting of heaven

a popular postcard entitled *The Poet*
I once sent to my sister

I wanted to become a woman
ashamed of her breasts

their enormous size
pendulous weight

I listened to her
undressing in the dark

afraid of how she will be
described

I am a paper hat
tumbling across a desert

On a dusty windshield
someone has scribbled

xylophone
blubber breath

dumbo and bud

Radiant Silhouette IV

Frenzy softens the air.

The hardly used desire was posted on the outer panel
of the blackboard sky. Beneath rows of illustrated
fragments, someone whispers and someone listens,
and no one agrees on how many were in the bed between
one and one equals all the hours you have known or
imagined knowing another.

The inside of the walls got sticky, and tiny spots of
pink paper floated toward the rain spattered clouds.

I followed feathers down flagpoles

I stood on trains,
   sat across from
     and beside

I traced the little wigs of a tarnished button,
   and started eating the perfumed crumbs
     left out for the leper of milk

I licked peeling canisters
   until rain trickled out of
     my mouth and pockets

I counted the insect vowels missing from the slag heap

I inserted a strip of imitation fur into the Book of Neon

After he tied her to the bed, she handcuffed him to the stove.
Dark aquamarine light slipped off the rounded edges of the
upturned venetian blinds, dropping into mirrors fastened
at the corners.

An old movie flickered on the outer border of their gnawed platform.

Radiant Silhouette V

Dear matted squirrel tongue
tendrils rise above our village

men bray at the prospect of
another coal hard dusk

children adore the bust
honoring the baby faced dictator

Dearest ape neck
why sigh in daylight

when there are kisses
you will always treat

like snakes
Fatima Fathead and Iron Josh

I lost the formula
after I followed the flagellants

to their weekly reception
and saw their treasurer

Darling hat rack
the destiny of children is postponed

I repeatedly coughed
in your rhinestone shoes

Another book of love poems
is stolen from the burning library

Dented dog dish
don't envy the esthete

in his firefly cell
Meet me behind

the Blue Hell Mambo Club
Former Lord of the Summer Purges

Fellow slime wallower
in the garden of earthly delights

Once I was as tender
as a broken wing

Postcard from Trakl

Memory's branch quivers
beneath the weight of a butterfly

How am I to know what it wants
without asking

Could it be that simple, the question
and then the answer

Why do we fall outside of these additions
or consult the zodiac surrounding us

read its rotten walls and bulb glare
Why substitute names for things

when the things name us
(our vowels and consonants)

into their sleep,
one from which they will never awaken

Am I just an echo drifting back to myself
who is sitting beneath the river

drinking air
Something must have told me to say this

A rock or the memory of a rock
falling toward the shadow it once owned

Acknowledgments

Grateful acknowledgment is made to the following for permission to print their copyrighted material:

Ai: "The Man with the Saxophone" reprinted from *Sin* (Houghton Mifflin, 1986) by Ai. Copyright © 1986 by Ai. "'The Shadowboxer" reprinted from *Fate* (Houghton Mifflin, 1991) by Ai. Copyright © 1991 by Ai. Reprinted by permission of Houghton Mifflin Company. All rights reserved.

Ali: "A Lost Memory of Delhi," "A Dream of Glass Bangles," "Cracked Portraits," and "Homage to Faiz Ahmed Faiz" reprinted from *The Half-Inch Himalayas* (Wesleyan University Press, 1987) by Agha Shahid Ali. Copyright © 1987 by Agha Shahid Ali. Reprinted by permission of University Press of New England.

Amirthanayagam: "The Elephants Are in the Yard" is reprinted by permission of the poet. Copyright © 1992 by Indran Amirthanayagam. "There Are Many Things I Want to Tell You" appeared originally in *The Kenyon Review* (Fall 1991) and is reprinted by permission of the poet. Copyright © 1991 by Indran Amirthanayagam. "So Beautiful" first appeared in *Catalyst* and is reprinted by permission of the poet. Copyright © 1992 by Indran Amirthanayagam.

Berssenbrugge: "Chronicle" reprinted from *Summits Move with the Tide* (Greenfield Review Press, 1974) by permission of the poet. Copyright © 1974 by Mei-mei Berssenbrugge. "The Constellation Quilt" reprinted from *Random Possession* (I. Reed Books, 1979) by permission of the poet. Copyright © 1979 by Mei-mei Berssenbrugge. "Tan Tien," "Jealousy," and "The Swan" reprinted from *Empathy* (Station Hill Press, 1989) by permission of the poet. Copyright © 1989 by Mei-mei Berssenbrugge.

Chang: "After the Storm," "Bamboo Elegy: Two," and "Near-Sightedness" reprinted by permission of the poet. Copyright © 1992 by Edmond Yi-Teh Chang.

Chin: "Exile's Letter *(Or: An Essay on Assimilation),* "Repulse Bay," and "American Rain" reprinted from *Dwarf Bamboo* (Greenfield Review Press, 1987) by permission of the poet. Copyright © 1987 by Marilyn Chin. "Barbarian Suite" reprinted by permission of the poet. Copyright © 1992 by Marilyn Chin.

Chock: "Working Construction," "Poem for George Helm: Aloha Week 1980," and "The Bait" reprinted from *Last Days Here* (Bamboo Ridge Press, 1990) by permission of the poet. Copyright © 1989 Eric Chock.